Granville Proprietary Land Office Records

- Volume #1 -

ORANGE COUNTY NORTH CAROLINA

Loose Papers

- 1752-1763 -

By:
William D. Bennett

Southern Historical Press, Inc.
Greenville, South Carolina

Copyright 1987
By: William D. Bennett, C.G.

Copyright Transferred 2018 to:
Southern Historical Press, Inc.

All rights reserved. No part of this publication may be reproduced, stored in a retrieval system, transmitted in any form, posted on to the web in any form or by any means without the prior written permission of the publisher.

Please direct all correspondence and orders to:

www.southernhistoricalpress.com
or
**SOUTHERN HISTORICAL PRESS, Inc.
PO BOX 1267**
375 West Broad Street
Greenville, SC   29601
southernhistoricalpress@gmail.com

ISBN #0-89308-994-X

Printed in the United States of America

INTRODUCTION

Many researchers feel at a dead-end when they find that there is a hiatus of most of the volumes of records normally searched such as Deed Books, Will Books, and Minutes of the County Court. In North Carolina, such is often not the situation. One such example is that of Burke County. Most references state that the records were burned by Federal troops in 1865. While it is true that the Will Books and Deed Books were destroyed, many of the Court Minutes survive, and it would appear that none of the loose papers were touched. Orange County provides another such example. In 1781, when Hillsboro fell to the British, James Munro, a Tory with a grudge against the State, seized the Deed Books and buried them. Not properly protected, the Deed Books rotted before they were recovered. Only one pre-Revolutionary War Deed Book of Orange County survives. Deed Book 2 also contains a few deeds from this period. The court minutes have also suffered a loss. But this should not act as a deterent for those wishing information from early Orange County. There are many sources other than county records which can be researched.

Orange County was formed in 1752 from the western part of Johnston, Bladen, and Granville Counties. It has been said that the county "was named in honor of William of Orange, who became King William III of England and saved the English people from the tyranny of James II." Professor William S. Powell states, "It has long been said that the county was named for Wiliam III (1650-1702) of the House of Orange, who ruled England from 1689 to 1702. However, in 1752 when the county was formed, the infant William V (1748-1806) of Orange was Stadholder, and his mother, Anne, daughter of George II of England, controlled affairs of state. It seems reasonable to assume that Orange County was named in honor of William V of Orange (and perhaps also to flatter his grandfather, George II of England) instead of for William III who had been dead for fifty years."

At its formation in 1752, Orange County included a major portion of the central Piedmont section of North Carolina. It encompassed present Caswell, Person, Durham, Orange, Alamance, and Chatham Counties and about half of Wake, Rockingham, Guilford, and Randolph Counties. The western boundary of Orange County had been established in 1750 with the formation of Anson County which described the line as running up Drowning Creek to its head, "then by a Line, to run, as near as may be, equidistant, from Saxapahaw (present Haw) River, and the Great Pee-Dee (present Yadkin) River. This line was altered in 1753, with the formation of Rowan County, to read "to begin where Anson Line was to cross Earl Granville's Line, and from thence in a direct line, North, to the Virginia Line." The act establishing Orange County provided that the eastern boundary begin "on the nearest Part of the Virginia Line to Hico Creek, thence a direct line to the Bent of Eno River, below the Occanechas, near to the Plantation where John Williams now dwelleth; thence down the South side of Eno River, to Neuse River; thence down Neuse River to the mouth of Horse Creek; thence a direct line to the Place where Earl Granville's Line crosses Cape Fear River." A year later (1753) the line was changed to a line beginning "on the Virginia Line, twenty Miles west of Granville Court House, running thence a South Course to Neuse River, thence bounded by said River to the Mouth of Horse Creek." The boundary between Orange and Johnston County (from Horse Creek to the Cape Fear River) was moved westward in 1761. It was defined as "a Line to begin at the South West Corner of Granville County and running thence to a due South Course to Johnston or Cumberland County Line, which of the said County Lines it may first intersect." This was the last change while the Grancville Land Office was open, the line was changed once more with the formation of Wake County in 1770. The description reads "then a straight line to Orange Line, at the lower end of Richard Hill's Plantation, on Buckhorn; then the same Course continued Five Miles; then to the corner of Johnston County on Granville Line." The southern boundary was always Earl Granville's Line and the northern boundary was the Virginia Line.

Prior to the formation of Orange County, there had been two major dispositions of land in the area. On 6 November 1727 Edward Moseley obtained a grant for 10,000 acres and on 28 November he obtained a second grant for 8,400 acres. On 10 April 1730 Lewis Conner obtained a grant for 10,000 acres. These grants lay in the Hawfields area, now Alamance County. After the deaths of Moseley and Conner, Governor Burrington obtained title to these three grants. On returning to England, financial problems caused Burrington to be sent to Debtor's Prison. To obtain the benefits of the Act of Parliament for insolvent debtors, Burrington turned all of his assets over to the court who assigned Lieutenant General John Guise, as greatest creditor, to adminster Burrington's assets. One of Burrington's creditors was Samuel Strudwick of New Hanover County, North Carolina. Strudwick held a mortgage on the Orange County lands for which two thousand and forty seven pounds eighteen shillings and four pence was owed. In a settlement with General Guise, Strudwick paid nine hundred fifty six pounds one shilling and eight pence and received title in fee simple to the Orange County lands. During the interim, a number of people had settled on this land. In 1768 Strudwick filed, and successfully prosecuted, ejectment suits against those settled on his property. The suits were not brought to a conclusion until the late 1780s. The Struther Ejectment Suits provide material for a study unto itself. The other major disposition of land in the area consisted of two of the twelve 100,000 acre tracts granted to Henry McCulloh by the King in 1737. This grant and McCulloh's sale of the land has been well covered by John Scott Davenport (North Carolina Genealogical Society Journal, Vol. IV, No. 2, p. 74).

When the Lords Proprietors sold the Carolina Grant to the King in 1729, Lord Carteret refused to sell his interest. In 1744 the King alloted Lord Carteret, later Earl Granville, his one eighth share of the colony. The Granville Grant was a sixty mile wide strip running from the Atlantic Ocean to the "South Seas" bordering on the Virginia Line. This included all vacant land in what was to become Orange County. The procedure for obtaining land from Granville began with filing an "Entry" briefly describing the tract of land desired and the number of acres. The grantee signed the Entry and on occasions also signed the Entry Book maintained by Granville's agents. The next step was to secure a "Warrant to the Surveyor" to have the land surveyed. This warrant gave the same information concerning the land as appeared on the Entry. The surveyor would then survey the land and return the Warrant with three copies of a plat of the land including the metes and bounds. Then two copies of the deed were prepared, signed by both Granville's agent and the grantee. One copy was for the grantee, the other for Earl Granville. A copy of the plat was attached to each copy of the deed. The third plat was filed with the Entry and Warrant and kept by Granville's agent. With the death of Granville in 1763, most of the Granville Proprietary Land Office Papers remained in private hands. In 1777 the General Assembly passed an act providing for the State to acquire all of these papers which had survived. It is apparent, from the record, that many of the papers had become scattered by this time. Those papers located were filed with the Secretary of State. Sometime during the early part of this century, probably when Bryan Grimes was Secretary of State, part of the collection came into the hands of the North Carolina Historical Commission and were eventually deposited at the North Carolina State Archives. In 1985 both collections were merged at the Archives.

Those papers needing it were laminated and the collection arranged by counties. All documents concerning a particular tract of land are filed in folders labeled with the name of the last known claimant to the land. These folders are arranged alphabetically within the county. It should be borne in mind that these papers could be assigned. Therefore it is possible to find that an Entry was made by one individual and assigned to a second individual in whose name the Warrant was issued. The warrant could be assigned to a third individual in whose name the Survey was made. The entire group of papers could be assigned to a fourth individual in whose name the deed was issued. You should also be aware that an individual did not have to live in the county to acquire a tract of land. The grantee may never have been in Orange County from the time the Entry was made, until he gets a deed, and then sells the tract. Only when the Entry, Warrant, or Survey actually state that a person was living on the land can you be sure that anyone listed in these papers was in Orange County. One other reference proves a person's presence in Orange County. Anyone listed as a chain bearer on the survey was on that tract at the date of the survey. In these abstracts I have used the following abreviations for the designation of chain bearers listed on the surveys. "CB" for chainbearer; "CC" for chain carrier; and "SCC" for sworn chain carrier. While it is normally thought that the designation "Sworn Chain Carrier" meant the individual was at least twenty one years of age, this was not always true. A sworn chain carrier was one who could testify in a court action. When a child reached the age of fourteen he was considered to have reached the "Age of Reason" and therefore knew the difference between right and wrong. For this reason, under certain circumstances, he wasallowed to testify in court. If the abstract indicates that more than one survey has survived in these papers, it is almost certain that no deed was issued for the land. In these abstracts, dates of entry, survey, and deed which follow the description of the land are dates which appear on the documents. Several years ago the North Carolina State Archives acquired the surviving copies of the deeds sent to Earl Granville. These are arranged in alphabetical order for the researcher. These papers have not been consulted in preparing this volume.

GUIDE TO THE MAPS

These maps are provided to aid the researcher in locating records for the area which became Orange County and its periphary. It should be borne in mind that when an area became part of a new county the old records did not follow to the court house of the new county. Therfore, the researcher needs to know what county exercised authority over the area during the time-frame of the research. These boundaries were determined from three sources. They are based on the actual acts of the General Assembly for the establishment of a county, or by implications of the acts establishing the counties or lateer counties, or from the implied boundaries based on actions of individuals at the time.

The 1725 map provides the implied boundaries at the time. I have found no evidence that either Bertie or Craven Preciincts attempted to exercise any authority in the area. Land grants in the Haw Fields area of present Alamance County designated the area only as "Bath County." The act establishing Bertie County gave the western boundary as "including both sides of said (Roanoke) River, and the branches thereof, as far as the limits of this government." Edgecombe County was formed from Bertie County and its southern boundary was described as "the Middle grounds between the Tar and Neuse River." This same boundary was given for the southern boundary of Granville County when it was formed from Edgecombe County. It should also be noted that the act establishing New Hanover Precinct in 1729 did not state tthat it was the southern part of Craven Precinct. The act reads, "That the Southern Part of the Province shall be erected into a Precinct." During the early years of the province, for convenience, the high ground between two major water courses was used as a dividing line between counties. This would appear to have been the situation with the Orange County area at a time when there was little or no settlement in the area.

Following the maps of the Orange County area is a map showing the lands granted to Edward Moseley and Lewis Conner. This map was prepared by Mile Philbeck for his book "Bladen County Land Grants." It was based on the survey made for Samuel Strudwick. Any one interested in the early land grants in the area should consult Philbeck's volume. There is also a map of the two tracts granted Henry McCulloh which were located in Orange County. This is based on a tracing of the original survey made for McCulloh. The tracing was made by Dr. Charles R. Holloman. I wish to thank the two men for the use of their material.

Lastly, there are Water Basin Maps of the rivers which drained the area. These were the Roanoke, Tar, Neuse, Cape Fear, and Yadkin Rivers. These maps were prepared from U.S. Geological Survey Maps of the area by the North Carolina Department of Natural Resources and Community Development, who granted permission for their use in this volume. Names of creeks and branches are those currently in use. It should be noted that many streams have changed names during the past two hundred years.

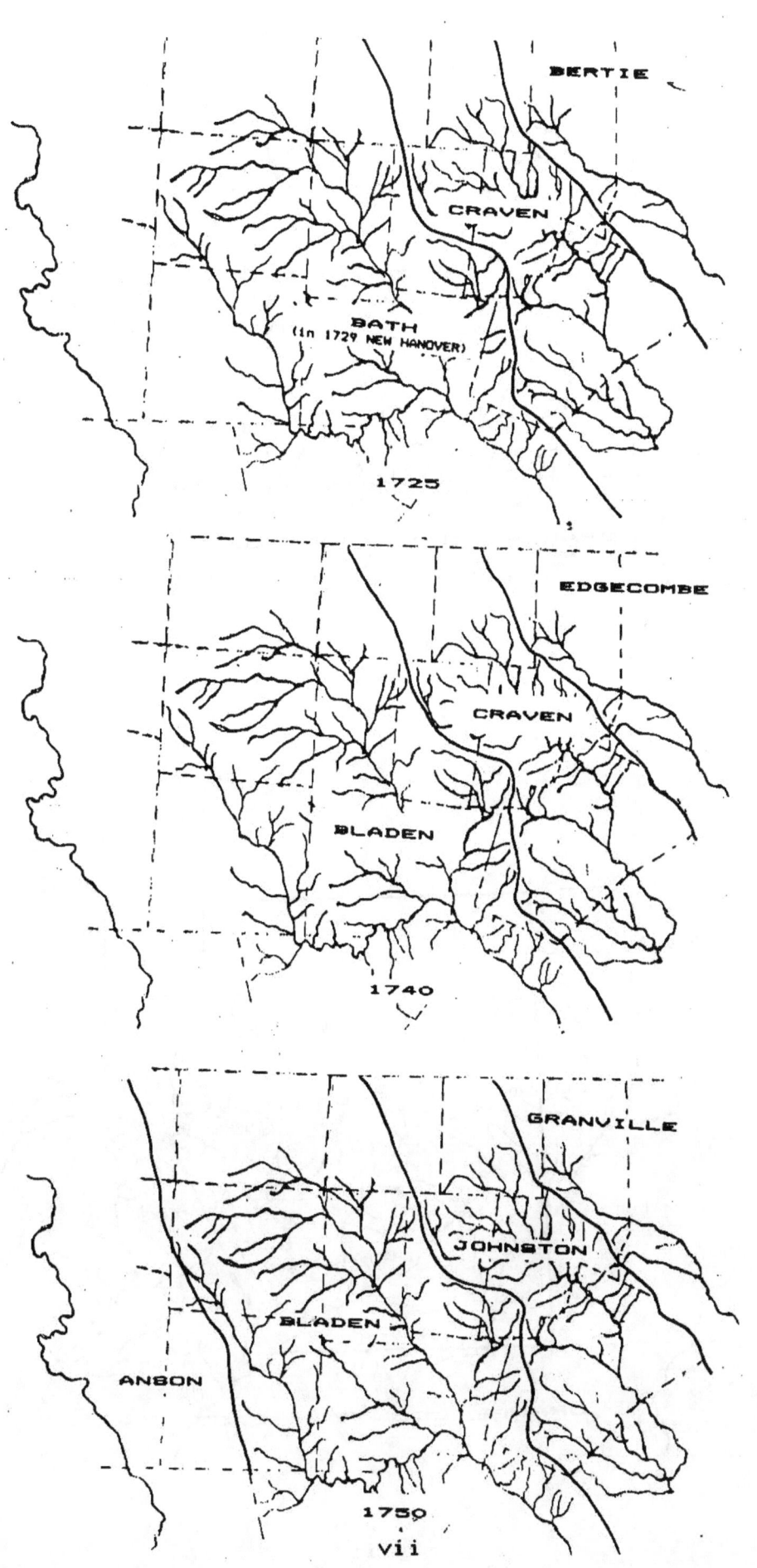

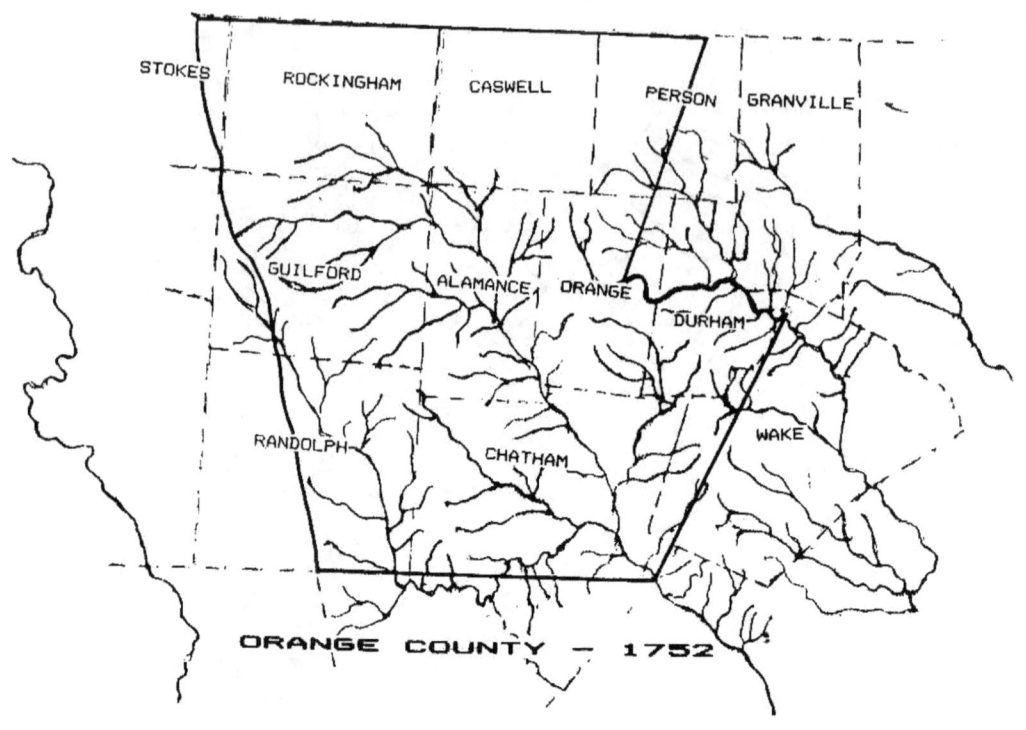
ORANGE COUNTY — 1752

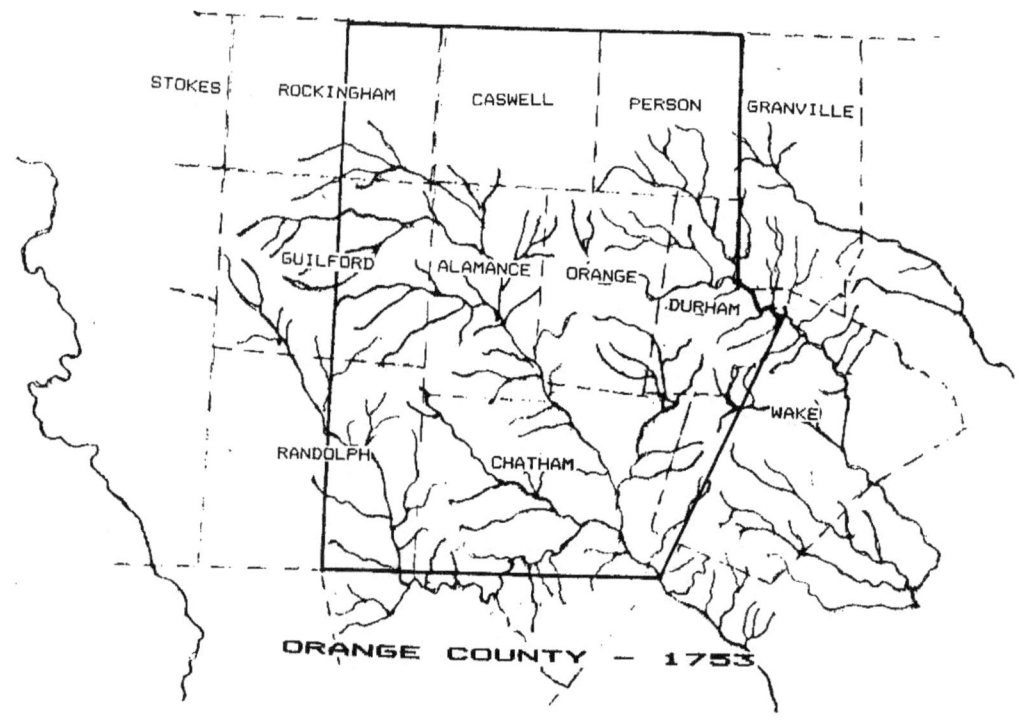
ORANGE COUNTY — 1753

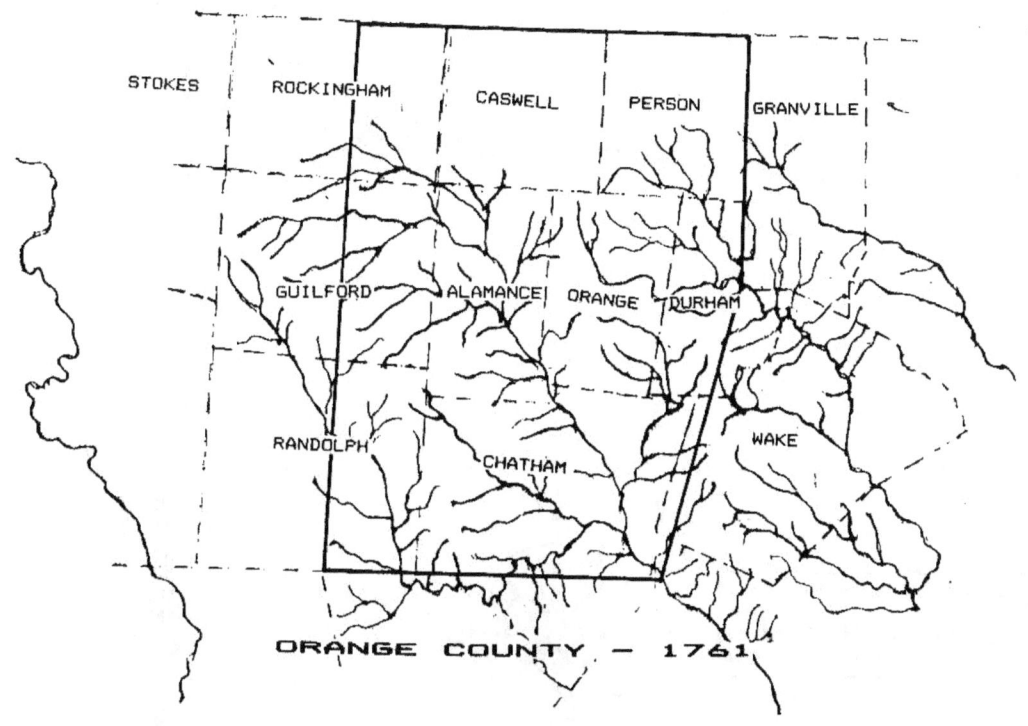
ORANGE COUNTY — 1761

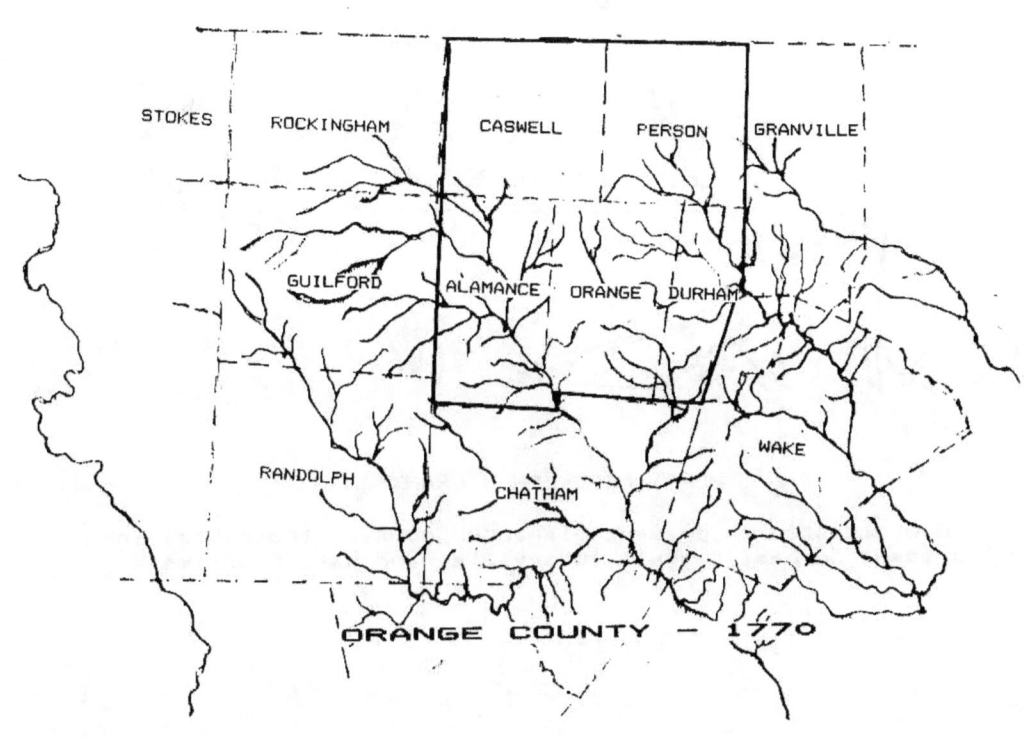
ORANGE COUNTY — 1770

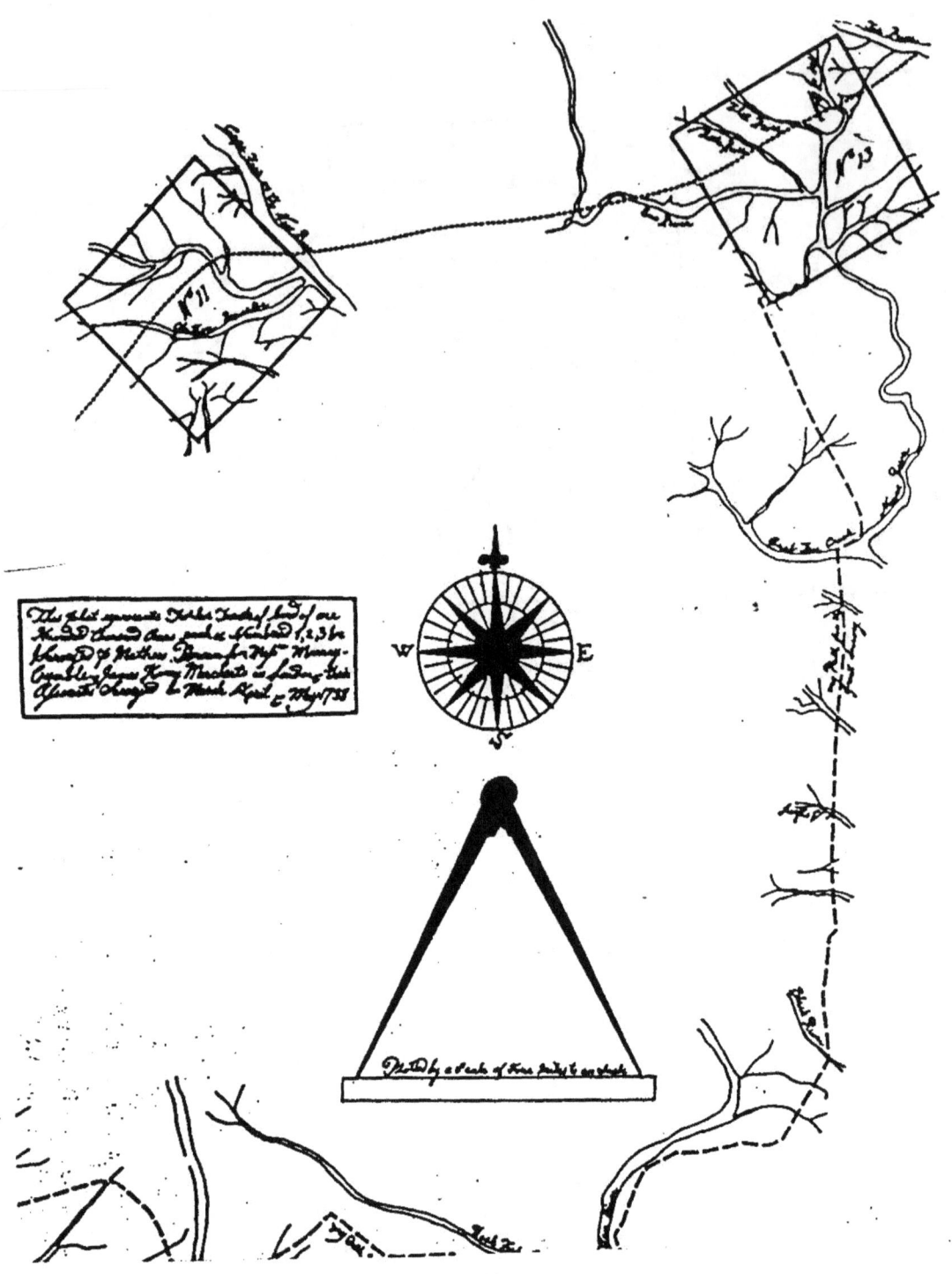

HENRY MCCULLOH"S GRANTS

(One located in present Alamance County, the other in present Durham, Caswell, Granville, and Wake Counties)

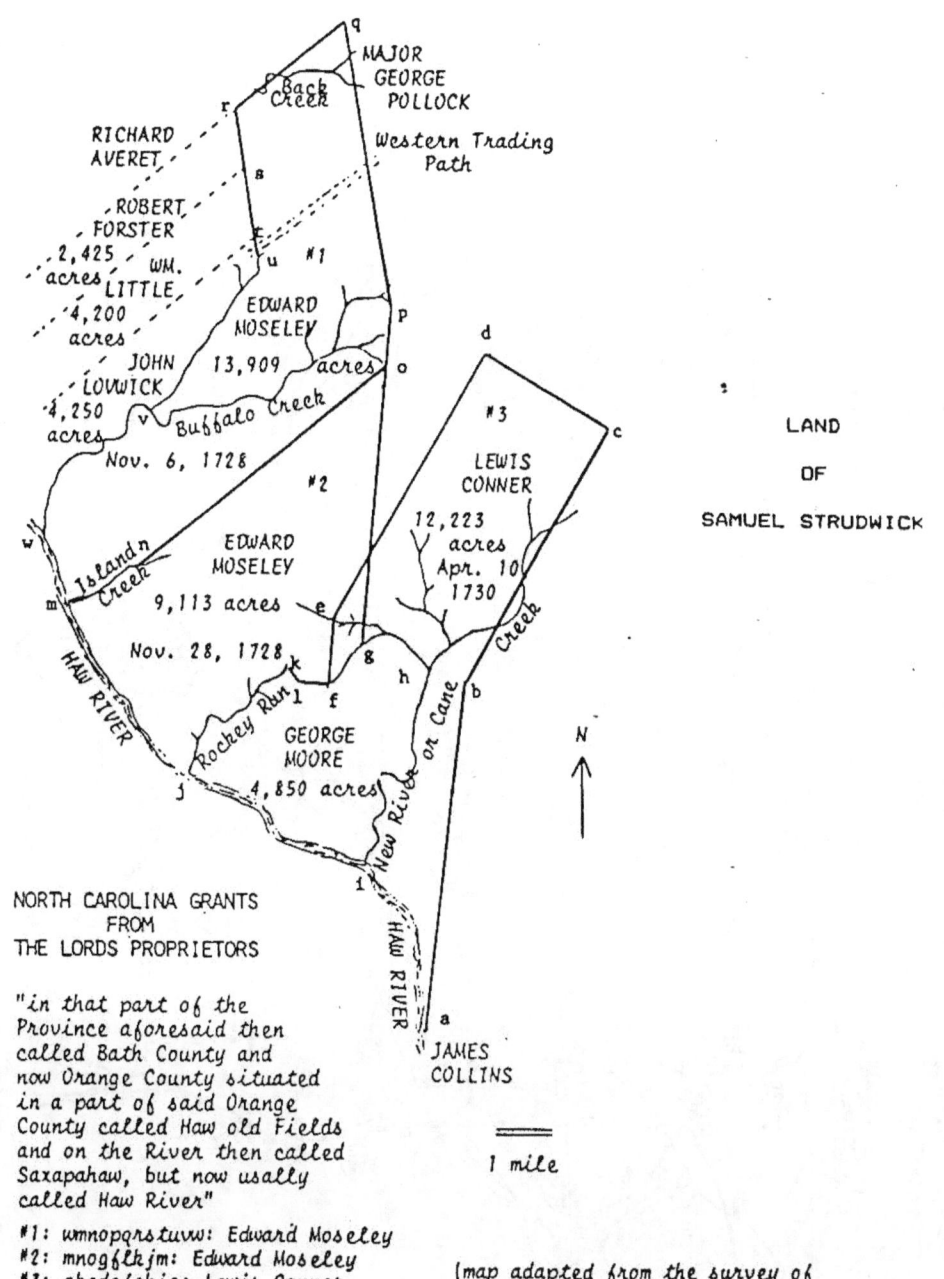

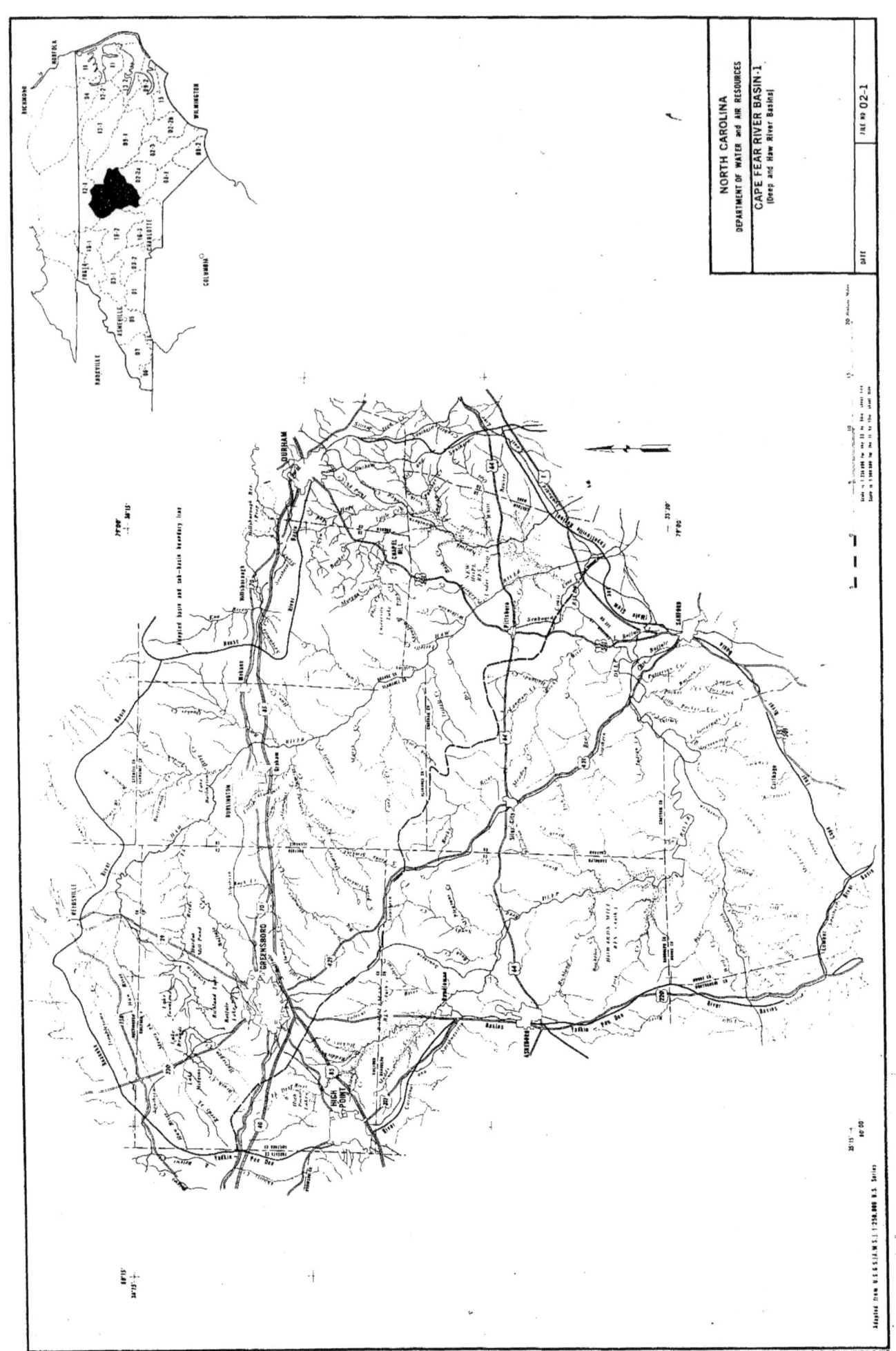

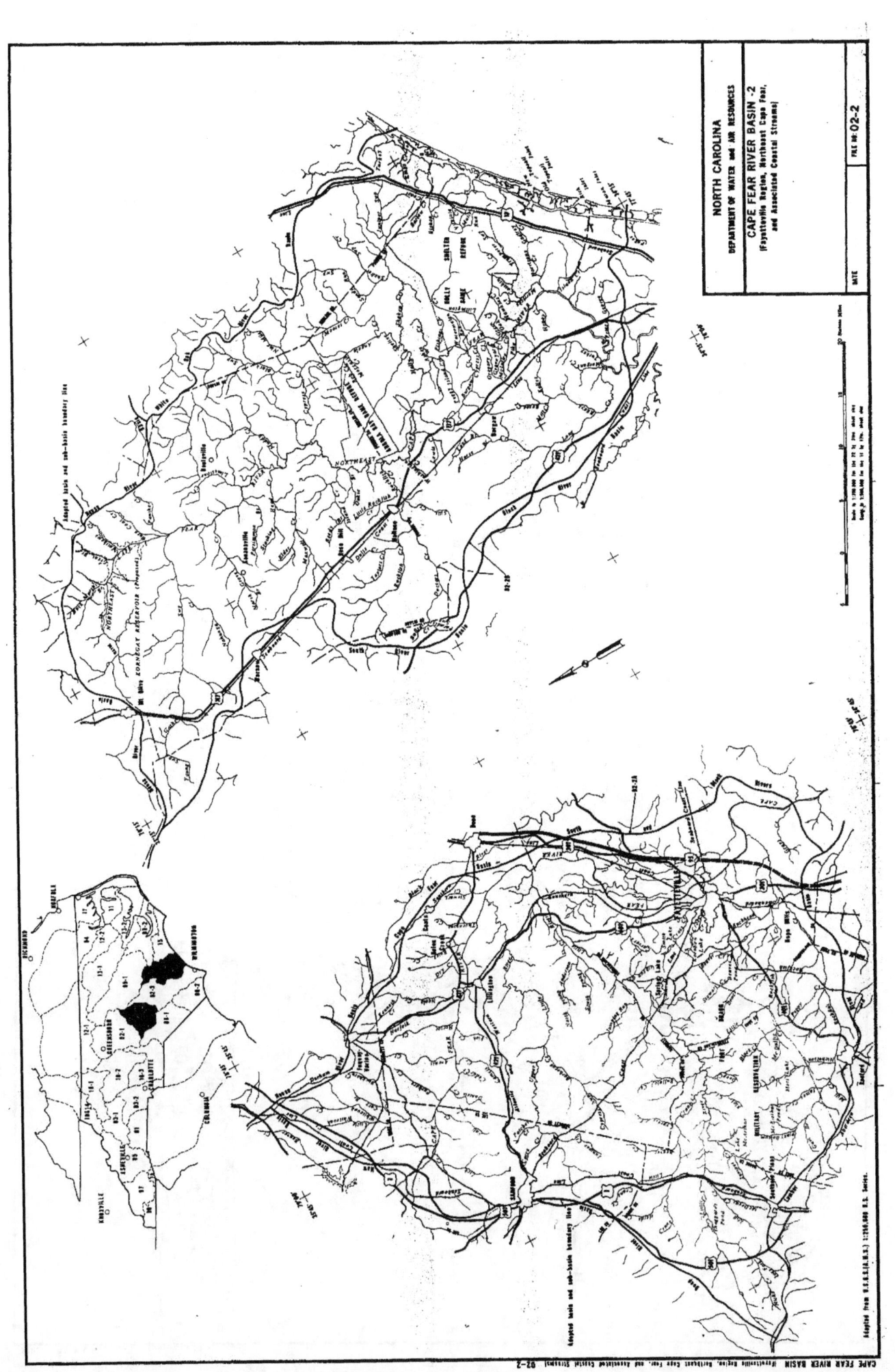

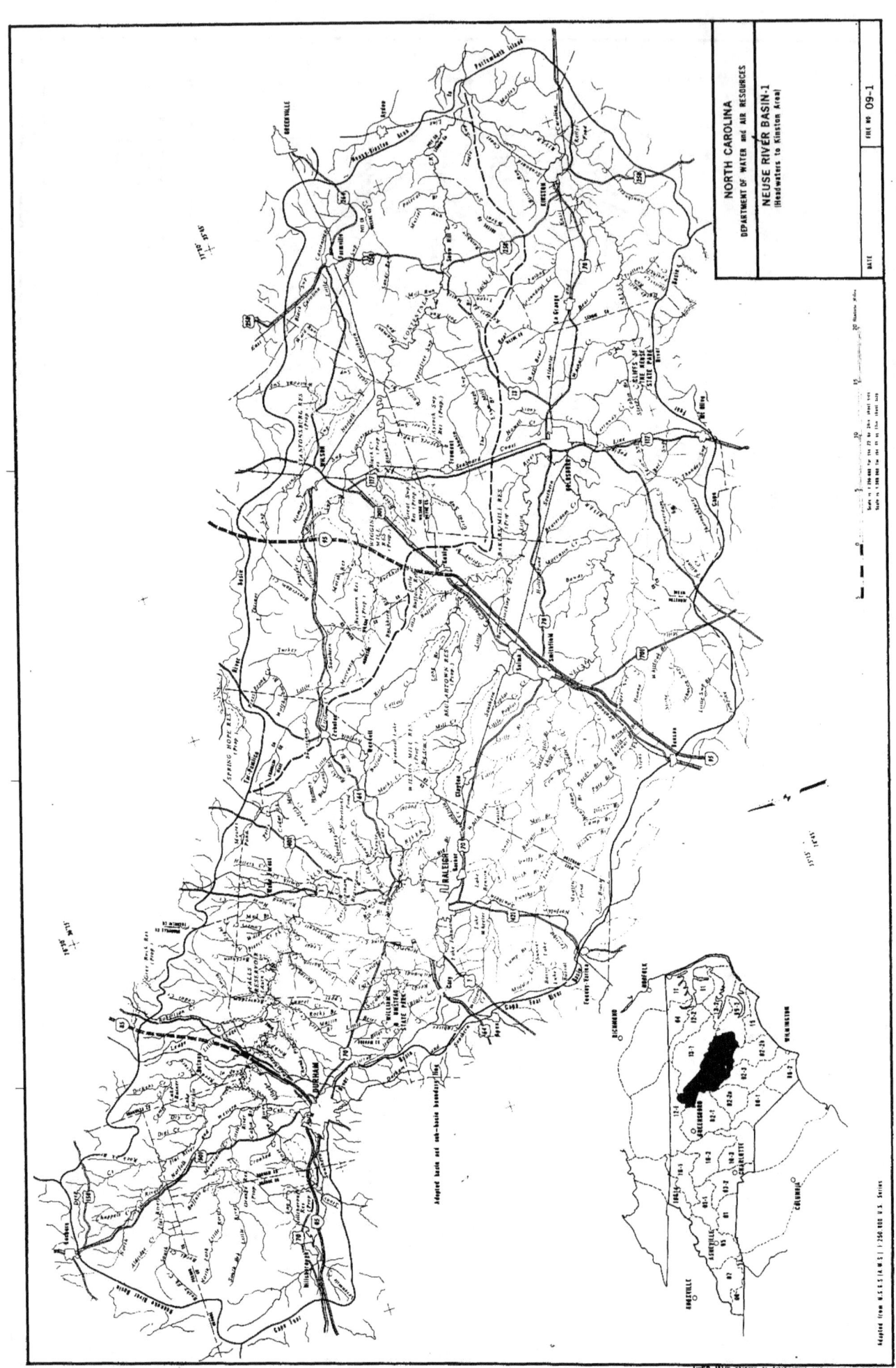

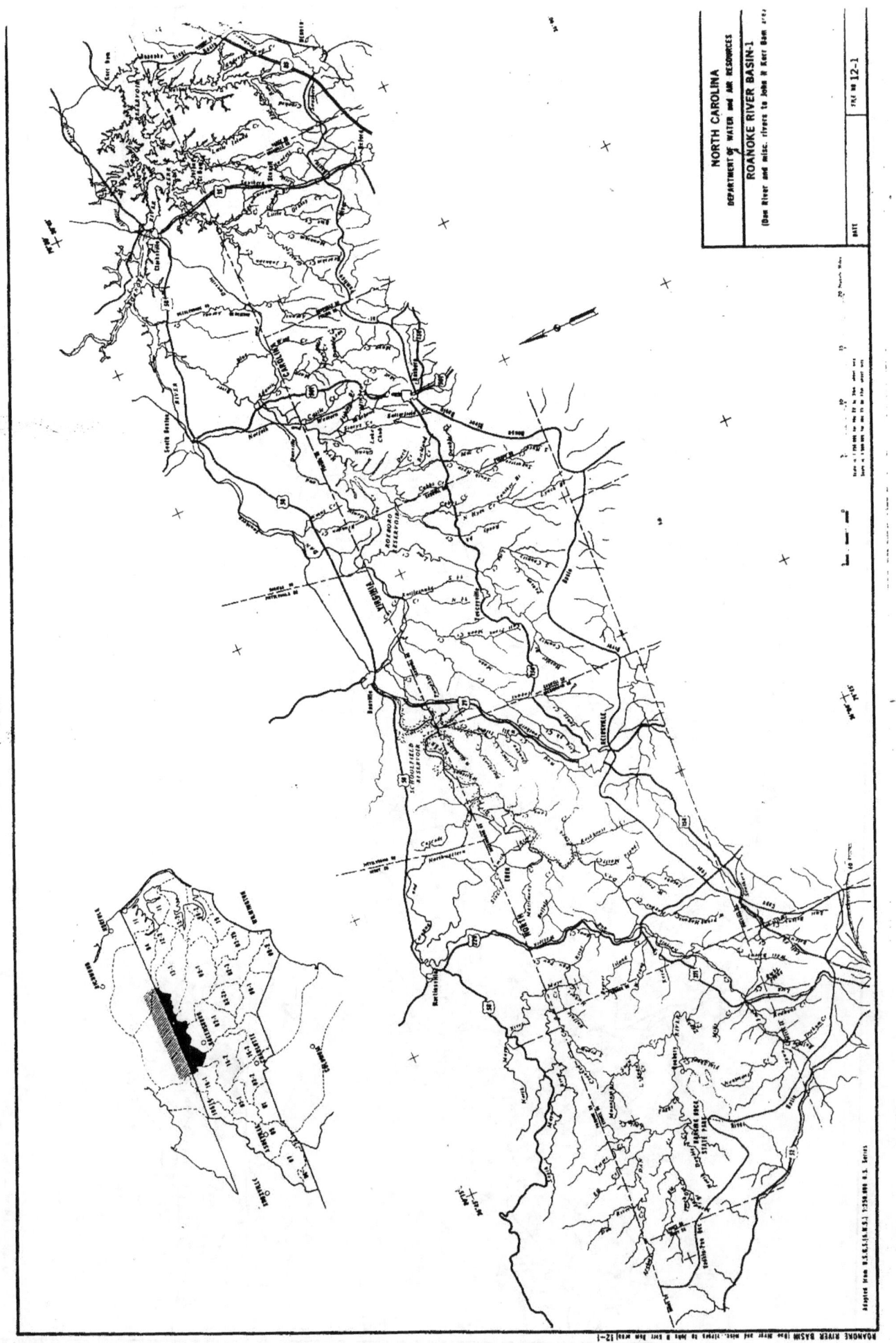

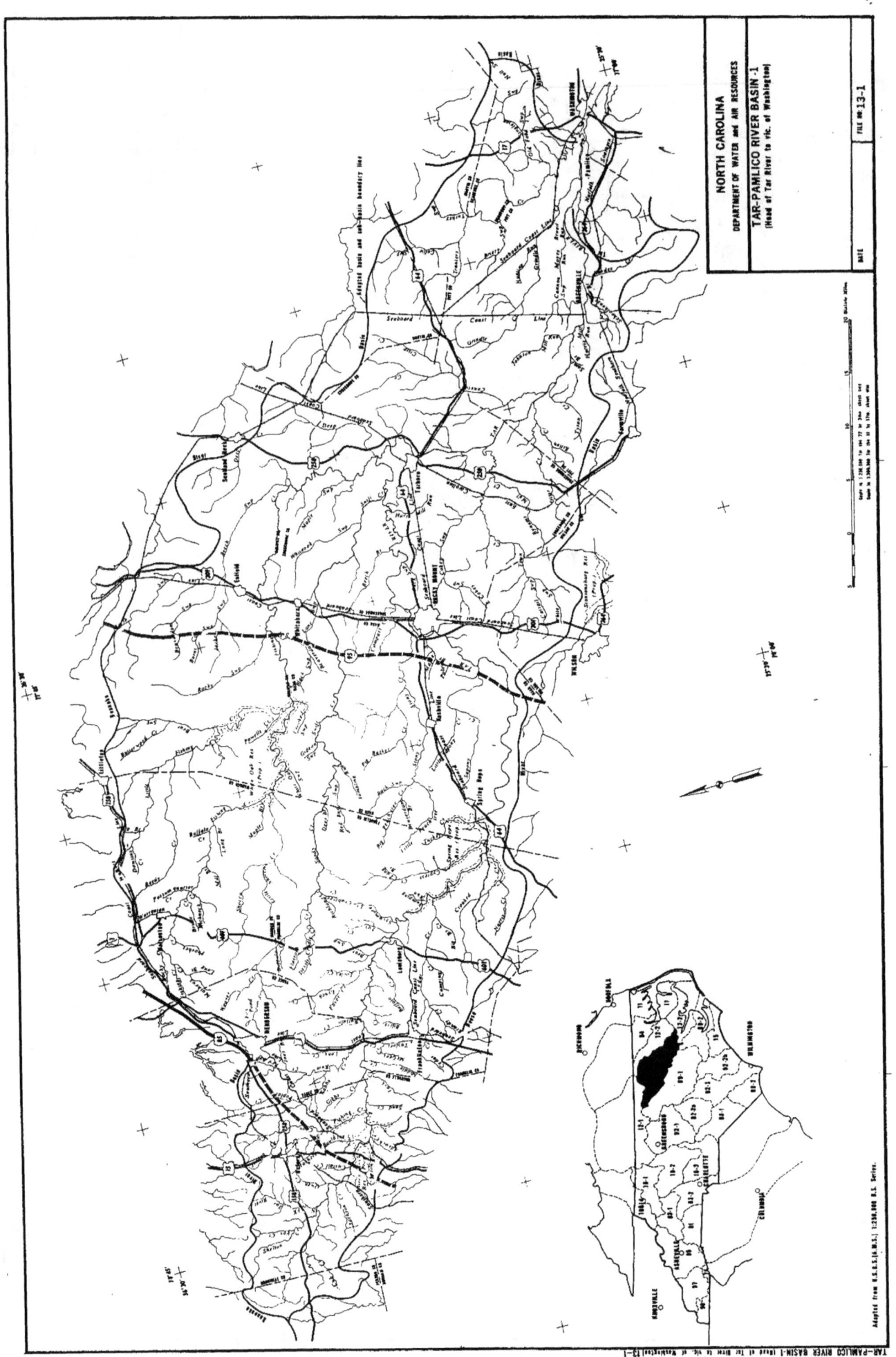

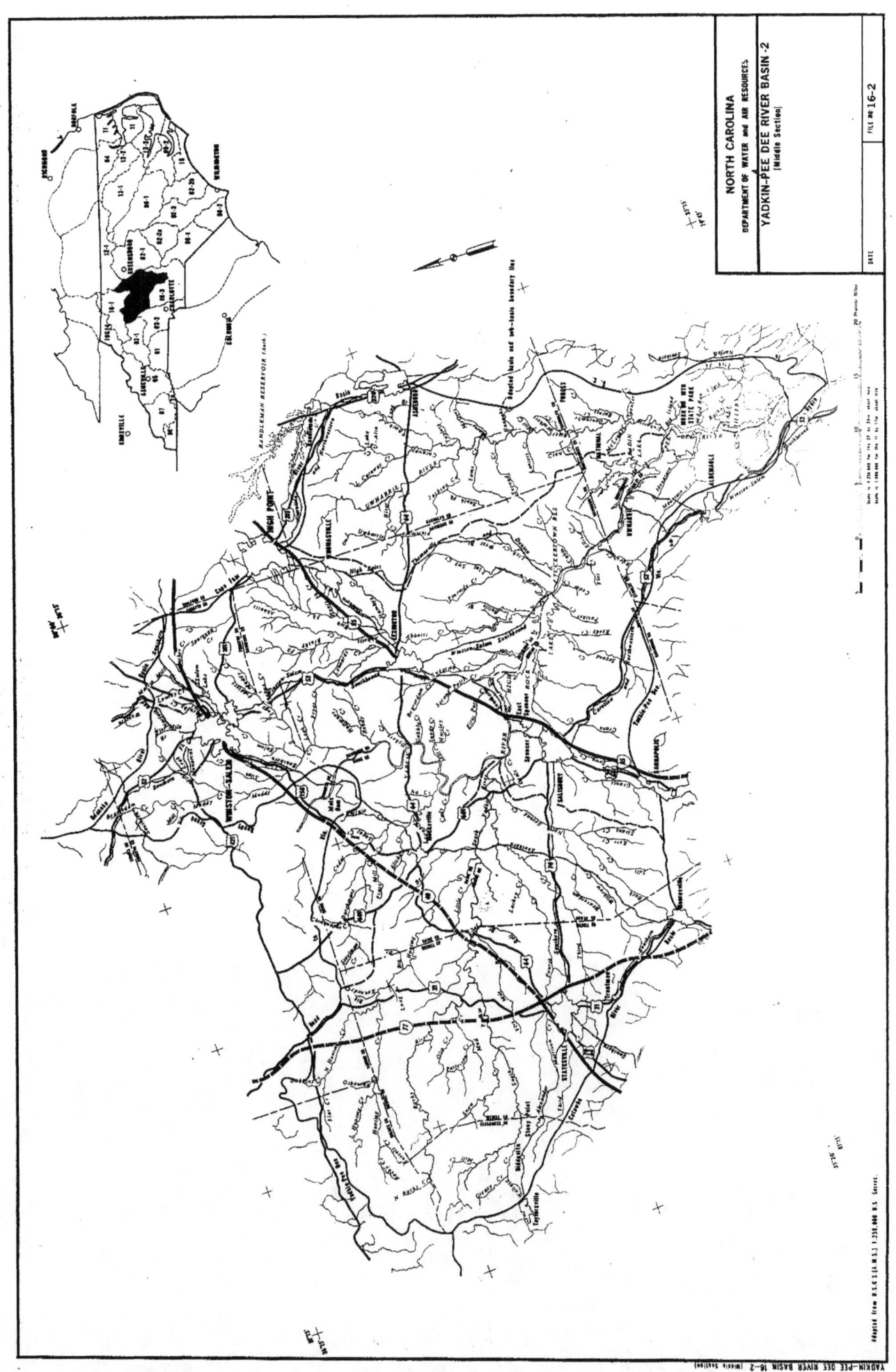

ABSTRACTS OF THE LOOSE PAPERS FROM THE
GRANVILLE PROPRIETARY LAND OFFICE
FOR
ORANGE COUNTY

Smith, John
    700 acres on Crabtree Cr.
    Entered 22 Aug 1761
    File envelope empty (#01337)

Barnett, Hugh   Survey   (Torn)
    150 acres on Blue Wing Cr.; Robert Danielson,
    Thomas Barnet: SCC.
    Entered 26 Oct 1753

Jones, Tignall   Warrant   (Torn)
    (Torn) south side Swift Cr.
    Entered 9 Nov 1756
    Deed 21 May 1762

Reed, William, Esq.   Survey   No Date
    240 acres on "Dreans of Enoe River"; joins Thomas Stubbs, Jack. Stubbs; John Dowell, Wm Reed
    Jnr: CC

Combs, William   Warrant   No Date
    400 acres on Mount (Walnut) Cr. on south side
    Wade's survey that William Wilkinson lives on.
    "removed on great Creek"
    Lost by McCulloghs signed over to James Hall"
    "Deed - In Thomas Wiley's name - 19 Feb 1760"

Tabor, John   Survey   2 (Torn)
    (Torn) acres; joins Phillip Pryor; Henry Ford,
    John Tabor, Sr., SCC.

Husband, Herman   Warrant   (Torn)
    Fragment of a warrant for 640 acres for land near
    Peter Youngblood and Great Shoals
    Entered 3 Nov 175? "In Lieu of an entry made 14
    November (?)"

Churton, William   Warrant   No Day or Month 175(Blank)
    640 acres; Begin above Nuse Path includes the
    Beaver Ponds.
    Entered 16 May 1752
    Deed 12 Nov 1756

Allen, John   Warrant   7 Apr 175(Torn)
    600 acres "on both sides of Creek joining John
    (Torn)ights uper line."
    Entered 28 Mar 1754
    "Cain Creek"
    Deed 20 Feb 1756

Collins, Dennis   Warrant   1 Aug 175(Torn)
    640 acres on both sides County Line Cr.; begins
    at the Fish Pot; joins Anne Merrett.
    Entered 14 Mar 175(Torn)
    Surveyed 10 June 1760
    Deed 29 Jan 1761

Harper, Robert   Warrant   Nov 175(Torn)
    400 acres on both sides Reedy Fk. of Hico.
    Entered 11 Jan 175(Torn)
    Assigned to Daniel Stillwell 19 Feb 1754 - Enoch
    Lewis, Wit.
    Deed 28 Apr 1756

Beasley, Henry   Warrant   Nov 175_(Torn)
    640 acres on the N. E. prong of New Hope; Begin at
    the lower end of an old beaver pond.
    Entered 26 Oct 175_(Torn)

Husband, Harman   Warrant   3 Nov 175(Torn)
    600 acres on Deep R. below Peter Youngbloods;
    joins Great Shoals.
    Entered 3 Nov 175(Torn)
    Deed 1 Aug 1760

Whitton, George by Ann Smith   Entry   19 Aug 176(Torn)
    700 acres on the Little Cr., waters of Deep R.;
    signed with a mark.

Clinten, Robert   Survey   6 Aug 1749(?)
    232 acres on Ellebees Cr.; Michael Wright, Thos
    Cammel, SCC.

Bridges, Joseph   Warrant   25 Apr 1751
    640 acres on south prong of Crooked Cr., on south

side of cr.
Entered 8 Feb 1750
Deed 9 Apr 1754

Lea, James   Entry or Warrant   3 Mar 1752
600 acres on Country Line Cr.
Original Papers Missing

Martin, Zachariah   Survey   26 May 1752
300 acres on north side of Haw R. on Terrills Cr.;
George Martin, William Martin CB; 3 copies

Martin, Zachariah   Survey   27 May 1752
573 acres on north side of Haw R. on Cain Cr. above the Piney Mountain; John Daniel, Hezekiah Collins CB: 3 copies.

Caswell, Richard   Survey   6 Oct 1752
320 acres on north side of Haw R. on upper side of Cain Cr. & both sides Great Road about a mile above John Hammonds. Chain Bearers names missing because of tear.

King, Peter   Warrant   5 Mar 1753
640 acres on both sides Prewels Fork near the head; includes waters of Troublesome Cr.
Entered 5 Mar 1752
Surveyed 1 Sept 1755
Deed 8 Jan 1761

Mills, William   Warrant   20 Mar 1753
300 acres joins John West, Senr.; on Stoney Cr.
Entered 9 June 1752
Deed 8 Jan 1761

Johnston, Henry   Warrant   20 Mar 1753
250 acres on both sides Eno R.; begin at Powel's line.
Entered 21 Jan 1752
Deed 15 Mar 1756

Kimbrough, Marmaduke   Warrant   20 Mar 1753
640 acres; fragment of warrant
Deed 1 Jan 1761

Jackson, Isaac   Warrant   20 Mar 1753
640 acres on both sides of Foresters Cr.; joins James Taylor's lower line
Entered 10 Oct 1752
Deed 19 Feb 1760

Sullivan, Owen   Warrant   20 Mar 1753
400 acres on Wm Rices line.
Entered 9 June 1752
Deed 1 Jan 1761

Pinson, Joseph   Warrant   20 Mar 1753
640 acres below Chavers on North Fk. of Haw R.; includes his improvements.
Entered 18 Dec 1751
Surveyed 6 Oct 1753
Deed 6 Sept 1754

Hill, Charles, for Pitman   Warrant   20 Mar 1753
640 acres on Main Fk. of Haw R.; includes Pitman's place.
Entered 2 Jan 1752
Deed - to Jno Pitman - 15 Mar 1756

Watson, James   Warrant   20 Mar 1753
400 acres joins the Governor's land; formerly supposed to be entered by Wm Moor; lying in Bucks Quarter
Entered 21 Jan 1752
Deed 13 Feb 1756

Rutledge, Reason   Warrant   20 Mar 1753
640 acres on the north fork of Belews Cr.
Entered 13 Jan 1753
"to be in the name of Patrick Hays"
Deed 18 July 1760

Gist, Nathaniel   Warrant   20 Mar 1753
640 acres on both sides the Town Fork Cr.; joins & below Wm Owens survey
Entered 27 Dec 1752
Deed 31 Dec 1760

Carmichael, John   Warrant   20 Mar 1753
640 acres on the Surra Town Fork Creek; joins Thomas Carmichael's entry.
Entered 27 Oct 1752
Surveyed 24 May 1753
Deed 31 Dec 1760

Fowler, Eliah   Warrant   20 Mar 1753
640 acres; begin in the fork of the river so running up both sides to include his own plantation.
Entered 23 May 1752
Deed to John Boyd for 424 acres
Deed 29 July 1760

Blackwood, William   Warrant   20 Mar 1753
500 acres both sides of Buffalo Creek; begin near the Indian field.
Entered 9 June 1752
Surveyed 9 Nov 1754 for 480 acres

Blackwood, William   Warrant   20 Mar 1753

640 acres on the fork of Barshears Creek; below Sam Hunter's entry.
Entered 1 Nov 1752
Surveyed for 640 acres

Goff, Henry   Warrant   20 Mar 1753
500 acres on northeast side of North West R. of Cape Fear; includes his improvements.
Entered 1 Nov 1753
"Laid out ye 18th of September 1753"
Deed 4 Nov 1756

Bullock, Richard   Warrant   20 Mar 1753
640 acres on Ellebees Cr.; begin on McCulloch's line.
Entered 26 Oct 1752

Carmicheal, William   Warrant   20 Mar 1753
640 acres on Surratown Fork; includes Charles Hoggan's improvements.
Entered 27 Oct 1752
Deed 31 Dec 1760

Dobbin, Hugh   Warrant   20 Mar 1753
640 acres Below Mr. Harper; both sides of County Line Cr.
Entered 23 May 1752

Stroud, John   Warrant   20 Mar 1753
640 acres near head of Oldfield Cr.; about 1/2 mile above old Field.
Entered 22 Jan 1753
Deed 23 Oct 1754

Wells, Joseph, Jr.   Warrant   20 Mar 1753
300 acres on north side Haw R., upon Brush Cr.; near head thereof.
Entered 1 Nov 1752
Deed 11 June 1754

Watson, James   Warrant   20 Mar 1753
200 acres in fork of Seven Mile Cr.; joins John Gray on west side; begin at the creek at Gray's corner.
Entered 28 Nov 1751
Deed 17 June 1754

Rhodes, John   Warrant   20 Mar 1753
640 acres on south fork of the northeast Branch of New Hope, which comes in against Beasleys.
Entered At Edgecombe 1 Nov 1752
Surveyed for 567 acres - 1754
Deed 6 Novv 1755

Holton, William   Warrant   20 Mar 1753
640 acres on both sides Tar R.; begin at mouth of Snow Cr.
Entered 30 Dec 1752
Surveyed 30 May 1753
"I doe hereby assign this within Entry to William Mullen and Requests that the same may be Taken out in the Said Mullen's Name - 30 May 1753 - William Holton - Wit: Nathell Gist, Enoch Lewis."
"Deed to Wm Haltam Mar 13th 1755"

Hampton, James   Warrant   20 Mar 1753
640 acres on both sides the Town Fork & both sides old field Creek.
Entered 3 Mar 1752

Ellison, Joseph   Warrant   20 Mar 1753
200 acres on Little R. on south fork; joins the Governor's land.
Entered 19 Jan 1753
Deed 12 Mar 1755

Hasting, Henry   Warrant   20 Mar 1753
300 acres on south of Eno; joins the Govrs., John Grays & Henry Simmons.
Entered 1 Nov 1752
Surveyed No Date
Deed 11 Nov 1756
On outside: "184 acres"

Jeffreys, Osborn   Warrant   20 Mar 1753
400 acres on Kemp Br. where Blalock's path crosses Lick Cr.
Entered 27 Oct 1752

Jeffreys, Osborn   Warrant   20 Mar 1753
640 acres on the three prongs of Bartons Cr. that Blalock's Mill is on; near mouth of sd prong.
Entered 27 Oct 1752
Laid out 7ber ye 11th 1753

Linval, Thomas, Junr   Warrant   20 Mar 1753
200 acres on middle fork of Boilen's Cr.; begin at the Bigg Meadow.
Entered 21 Mar 1752
Deed 2 July 1760

Comb, William   Warrant   20 Mar 1753
700 acres on branches of Bogg Cr.; joins Thomas Nelson
On Little Creek.
Entered 16 May 1752
Surveyed for 348 acres
Deed 12 Nov 1756

Synnot, Michael   Warrant   26 Mar 1753

400 acres on Eno R; begin at mouth of Seven Mile Cr.
Entered 19 Jan 1753
Deed 13 Mar 1755

Jeffreys, Osburn   Warrant   13 Apr 1753
640 acres joins & around his own patent land on Flatt R.
Entered 8 May 1753
Surveyed 12 Oct 1753
Deed 8 May 1756

Rhodes, William   Warrant   26 Apr 1753
640 acres on north side Haw R.; Begin at a large Branch.
"Removed to Bakers Cr. at a place that was formerly called Baker Cabbin"
(429 acres?)
Deed 11 May 1757

Blalock, John   Warrant   26 Apr 1753
300 acres; Begin in fork of Barton's Cr. & runs west.
Entered 26 Apr 1753
Deed 26 Oct 1754

Vandike, Henry   Warrant   27 Apr 1753
640 acres on Ellebees Cr. above Richard Bullock.

Parker, Richard   Warrant   27 Apr 1753
500 acres on east side New Hope Cr.; near & above his own land.
Entered 27 Apr 1753
Surveyed 21 Sept 1753
Deed 25 Oct 1754

Horton, James   Warrant   30 Apr 1753
400 acres on west side Mountain Br. below John Brown entry
Entered 19 Apr 1753

Bumpass, Samuel   Warrant   30 Apr 1753
400 acres; begin at the first br. that goes into Deep Cr. it being the branch that goes into the Mudd Br. that goes into Deep Cr. it being the br. that the path crosses from Bumpas to Gibson Mill
Entered 7 Mar 1753
Surveyed 15 Oct 1753
Deed 31 Dec 1760

Horton, James   Warrant   2 May 1753
640 acres on Dyals Cr begin a little above Capt. McCullogh Line
Entered 16 May 1752
Deed 24 July 1760

Hargrove, Richard   Warrant   2 May 1753
300 acres on North Fork of Haw R. on south side the fork; begin a half mile above Moreland Cabbin
Entered 6 Dec 1751
Deed 3 Aug 1760

Rutledge, Reason   Survey   5 May 1753
320 acres on north fork of Belews Cr.; Jno Rutledge, Moses Watson: SCC

Brooks, John, Esq.   Warrant   15 May 1753(1755?)
600 acres on Tick Cr., on south side Rocky R.
Entered 9 May 1753(1755?)
Surveyed 15 Apr 1756 for 639 acres
Deed 23 May 1758

Linvall, Thomas, Jr.   Survey   16 May 1753
200 acres on middle fork of Belews Cr.; begin below the great meadow; Thos. Linvall, Senr., Wm Linvall: SCC.

Linvall, Thos., Senr.   Survey   17 May 1753
200 acres on both sides Belew's Cr.; Wm Barclay, Wm Linvall: SCC.
Entered 21 Apr 1752

Gist, Nathaniel   Survey   19 May 1753
348 acres on both sides Town Fork Cr.; Jas Hampton, Jno Runnels: SCC
Entered 27 Dec 1752

Carmicheal, Willm   Survey   22 May 1753
330 acres on both sides Townfork Cr.; Jno Carmicheal, Jas Bedford: CB.
Entered 27 Oct 1752

Carmichael, John   Survey   24 May 1753
460 acres on both sides of Town Fork Cr.; joins Thos. Carmichael; Thos Carmichael, Jos Carmichael: SCC.
Entered 27 Oct 1752

Sullivant, Owen   Survey   4 June 1753
453 acres on both sides Matrimony Cr.; joins William Rice; Wm Hopper, Wm Lucus: SCC
Entered 9 June 1752.

Murdah, James   Survey   7 Oct 1753
331 acres on both sides the north fork of Little R.; joins Wm Aldridge; Patrick Rutherford, Jno Murdah: SCC.

Bumpass, Samuel   Survey   15 Oct 1753
218 acres on the Spring Br. that leads into Mud Br.; Wm Byas, Jno Bumpass: SCC.

Entered 7 Mar 1753

Barnett, Hugh   Warrant   26 Oct 1753
   300 acres on both sides Bluewing Cr.; includes
   Robert Southerland's Cabbin.
   Surveyed 26 Oct 1752(?)
   Deed 1 Aug 1760

Teat, Joseph   Warrant   3 Nov 1753
   640 acres on both sides Dan R.; begin at mouth of
   Mackey Cr.
   Entered 5 Mar 1753
   Deed 27 June 1759

Sorral, Samuel   Warrant   3 Nov 1753
   300 acres on both sides S. Hico; includes mouth of
   Double Cr.
   Entered 3 Dec 1751
   Surveyed for 422 acres
   Deed 12 Nov 1756

Churton, William, Esq. Warrant   3 Nov 1753
   640 acres in Orange & Johnston on both sides of a
   small cr. about 2 miles on the south side of
   Crabtree Cr, on both sides of the county line.
   Entered 3 Nov 1753 in lieu of an entry made 17 Dec
   1751
   Survey is on reverse side

Dobbin, Hugh   Warrant   3 Nov 1753
   640 acres on both sides of County Line Cr.
   Entered 13 Jan 1752
   Deed 6 May 1756

Deason, Benj.   Warrant   3 Nov 1753
   300 acres on south side of Dan R.
   Entered 31 Oct 1751
   Deed 12 Nov 1756

Lee, John   Warrant   3 Nov 1753
   640 acres on south Hico Cr.; at mouth of Rich Land
   Cr.
   Entered 11 Jan 1752
   Deed 8 May 1755

Kate, John   Survey   4 Dec 1753
   227 acres on south side of south fork of Flatt R.;
   joins James Dicken; Thomas Cates, Dennis Collins:
   SCC

Dickson, Michael   Survey   7 Dec 1753
   330 acres on Jest's Cr. adjoining Barnet's line;
   Robt Dickson, Henry Dickson: SCC
   Deed 29 July 1760

Martin, Zach   Warrant   10 Dec 1753
   640 acres on south side Deep R.; includes the plantation where Gilbert Patterson lives.
   Entered 1 Nov 1753
   Deed 1 Nov 1755

Mote (Mole), Jona Warrant   10 Dec 1753
   640 acres on James Collins Mill Cr.; includes fork
   and both sides of Main Creek.
   Entered 11 June 1753

Morris, Henry, Jr. Warrant   10 Dec 1753
   640 acres upon the head of Marks Cr. waters of New
   Hope; begin about a half mile below the Old Field.
   Entered 14 May 1753
   Surveyed 16 Oct 1755
   Deed 2 Aug 1760

Watson, James   Warrant   10 Dec 1753
   640 acres lying between the late Gov. Line the
   head of Sprit Br. & head of Stroud's Br.
   Entered 9 May 1753
   Apparently assigned to William Churton

Churton, William   Warrant   10 Dec 1753
   640 acres on south side Haw R.; joins William
   Carrol Place & to include Kenady Place.
   Entered 19 June 1753
   Deed 13 Mar 1755

Churton, William   Warrant   10 Dec 1753
   640 acres on both sides Enoe R.; joins on the low
   side of Jas Watson Entry whereon Gose lives; joins
   Jno Reed & where the Old Trading Path Crosses the
   Enoe.
   Entered 1 Nov 1753

Boyd, John   Warrant   10 Dec 1753
   640 acres on fork of Little Troublesome a branch
   of Haw.
   Entered 20 June 1753
   Surveyed for 630 acres
   "1 Apr 1754 - This entry being lost by a prior
   warrant of Peter King removed to the mouth of
   Little Troublesome"
   Deed 15 July 1760

Dobbin, Hugh   Warrant   10 Dec 1753
   640 acres; Begin on upper line of entry he made on
   Hogans Cr.
   Entered 19 June 1753
   Deed 7 Aug 1760

Boyd, John   Warrant   10 Dec 1753
   640 acres on north side Haw R.; about 3 miles above

Aron Pinson Mill; at mouth of Brashere Cr.
Entered 20 June 1753

Stroud, John, Jr.   Warrant   10 Dec 1753
640 acres; joins Thos. Lloyd on Benj. Bowlins Cr.
Entered 15 May 1753
"Orange 1 Octor 1754 It is this Day Agreed That the within warrt was obtained by John Stroud only in to Sd Loyd -John Stroad, Junr."

Nelson, Samle.   Warrant   10 Dec 1753
640 acres lying on Wm Miers & David Miers & on Jno Williams Hog Stock Br., waters of Mill Cr., waters of Haw R.
Entered 11 Sept 1753

Hart, James   Warrant   10 Dec 1753
320 acres on west side Enoe R.; joins the Gov. line & Jas Taylor.
Entered 18 May 1753 at Edgecombe
"now Jas Taylor"
196 acres
Deed 23 May 1758

Haywood, Col. Jno.   Warrant   10 Dec 1753
640 acres; Begin the lower end of the wide low ground of the Middle Fork of Belews Cr.; about 3 miles above Thos Linval Jr. survey.
Entered 20 June 1753
Deed 30 Apr 1754

Kimbrough, Marmaduke   Survey   10 Dec 1753
640 acres on Turkey Br. & Buckhorn Br.; Thomas Grimes, Phillip Howard: CB.

Boyd, John   Warrant   10 Dec 1753
640 acres on east side Main Fork of Haw R.; at mouth of Polk Br.
Entered 18 May 1753
Deed 15 July 1753

Potter, Ephriam   Warrant   11 Dec 1753
640 acres on both sides Wolf Island Cr.; about 10 miles above Jones Lan(torn); includes Thrashers Fork.
Entered 3 June 1753
Deed 20 Feby(torn)

Reed, Jno.   Warrant   11 Dec 1753
640 acres on that branch of Little R. that John Wades Mill is seated on; begin at a wt oak near where Parsons Cabbin was built.
Surveyed - No Date

Churton, Willm   Warrant   11 Dec 1753
700 acres on both sides Enoe R. & where the Trad-
Entered 11 Dec 1758

Horton, James   Survey   19 Feb 1754
320 acres on both sides Dials Cr.; Jas Wilkinson, Zachy. Downs: SCC

Horton, James   Survey   20 Feb 1754
482 acres on both sides Mountain Cr.; Joins John Wade; James Wilkinson, Zachy. Downs: SCC

Jones, John   Warrant   1 Mar 1754
640 acres "lying on both sides of Middle Branch that runs into Cain Creek the waters on the south side of Haw River including Jas Williams improvements."
Entered 14 Feb 1754

Dennis, John   Warrant   17 Apr 1754
350 acres on both sides Buck Quarter; adjoins Isaac Jackson.
Entered 21 Jan 1754
Surveyed for 507 acres.

Loyd, Thos Junr   Warrant   17 Apr 1754
640 acres on both sides Mark Morgan Creek on the upper side of the Piney Mountain near head of Morgan Cr.
Entered 17 Jan 1754
Surveyed 17 Oct 1755
Deed 12 May 1757

McFastern, Willm   Warrant   17 Apr 1754
400 acres on both sides Toms Cr.; includes the horseshoe bottom; on south side Deep R.
Entered 4 Mar 1754
Deed (480 acres) - 20 Feb 1756

Dickson, Simond (Simon) Warrant   17 Apr 1754
640 acres on both sides Cain Cr.; joins Anthony Chamney; includes his own improvements.
Entered 20 Mar 1754
Deed 15 Mar 1756

Hightower, Austin   Warrant   17 Apr 1754
640 acres on south fork of Morgan Cr. a little below the Great Falls near Mr. Caswell's upper line.
Entered 14 Jan 1754
Deed 2 Aug 1760

Brashear, Bazil   Warrant   17 Apr 1754
640 acres on south side of Haw R.; begin against the Piney sholes.
Entered 14 Jan 1754

Surveyed 12 Nov 1754 to his son Middleton Brashear
Deed 3 Feb 1761

Fershere, Charles (Foushee?)   Warrant   17 Apr 1754
640 acres "Lying about four miles of Haw River on the South side of Robinson Creek including Copelands improvement the place where he now lives."
Entered 15 Feb 1754
Surveyed 31 Mar 1756
Deed 7 Aug 1760

Barnes, Brinasely   Warrant   17 Apr 1754
640 acres on both sides Rocky R., at mouth of Mudlick Cr.
Entered 20 Mar 1754
Surveyed 5 Apr 1756

Davidson, John   Warrant   17 Apr 1754
640 acres; Begin at a white oak marked I D; run down Haw River on both sides to include his improvements. On reverse "near the Haw River Pond."
Entered 4 Mar 1754

Hall, James   Survey   20 Apr 1754
560 acres on north side of Enoe & both sides the Trading Path; joins Col. Corbin, Will Reed, & Thos. Wiley; Fredrick Natt, Wm Combs: SCC

Evans, Jacob   Warrant   26 Apr 1754
640 acres on Deep R.; includes his former survey.
Entered 26 Apr 1754
Deed 7 Aug 1760

Martin, John   Warrant   13 June 1754
640 acres on New Hope Cr.; includes Wm Gibson's improvements.
Entered 1 Apr 1754
Surveyed 26 Mar 1756
Deed 15 July 1760

Martin, John   Warrant   13 June 1754
640 acres; joins Zachariy Martin; on south side Haw R.; includes Mullen's Cabbin.
Entered 1 Apr 1754
Surveyed 29 Mar 1756 for 520 acres
Deed 15 July 1760

Kennedy, William   Warrant   13 June 1754
640 acres; joins Benjamin Bowlin on Wilkinson Cr, waters of New Hope Cr.; includes Prestwoods improvements.
Entered 1 Apr 1754
Surveyed 26 May 1755
Deed 6 May 1756

Landrum, John   Warrant   28 Aug 1754
640 acres; joins his former entry.
Entered 28 Aug 1754
Deed - No Date
"Haw River"

McCallaster(McCallester), James   Warrant   28 August 1754
300 acres on Tapleys Cr.; joins McCarver's entry; cross Little R.
Entered 2 July 1754
Surveyed for 640 acres
Deed 22 Feb 1759

Churton, William   Warrant   28 Aug 1754
640 acres on west side Haw R., both sides the Trading Path, begin where Nathan Ward formerly lived; joins the lines commonly called McCullock's lines.
Entered 28 Aug 1754 - In lieu of an Entry lost, Patented by Judge Smith, now in Mr. Rutherford's Possession.

Benton, Samuel   Warrant   28 Aug 1754
300 acres on North Fork of Crabtree Cr. joins his own upper line
Entered 28 June 1754 - Assigned to Nathaniel Kimbrough

Long, William   Warrant   28 Aug 1754
640 acres on west side Eno R.; joins the south side of James Taylor.
Entered 22 July 1754
Deed - to Joseph Sharp - Feb 1761

Cate, Thomas, Jr.   Warrant   28 Aug 1754
640 acres on both sides of Ellerbys Cr. at the fork including the Great lick below James Bowies plantation.
Entered 23 July 1754
"Removed to a fork of Cane Cr. 24 Sept 1755"

Cate, Thomas, Jr.   Warrant   28 Aug 1754
640 acres on both sides Cain Cr includes Robert Cate & Thos. Cate Sr. improvements about a mile below where the new road crosses Cain Cr.
Entered 23 July 1754
Deed 1 Mar 1759

Cantrell, John   Warrant   28 Aug 1754
300 acres on the head of Jordan Br. and Country Line Cr. being the place where Jonathon Motte planted a few hills of corn.
Entered 2 July 1754
Assigned to Isaac Cantrell
Surveyed 1 July 1755

Deed 13 Nov 1754

Vernall, William   Warrant   28 Aug 1754
620 acres on head of Vernall's Cr.; joins Timothy Terrell.
Entered 2 July 1754
Deed 11 Nov 1756

Standfield, John   Warrant   28 Aug 1754
500 acres on waters of Sandy Cr.; joins Zachariah Martin's land that he sold to Hugh Tollens at Mount Pleasant.
Entered 9 July 1754
"To be removed to the of Vernon Creek that runs into Rocky River between Timothy Terrel & Jno Landrum being the place where the schoolhouse stood."

Moss, James   Warrant   28 Aug 1754
640 acres on both sides Cain Cr.
Entered 23 July 1754
"Lost by John Martin - Entry removed to Stones Creek at the mouth running Down both sides the River Enoe 4 Nov 1754 - NB Leaving out Thos Nelson Emprov. - Moss to Thos. Nelson."
Surveyed 8 June 1757

Hatley, John   Survey   29 Aug 1754
382 acres on both sides Bush Cr., waters of New Hope; Robert Patterson, Charles Carter: CB.

Boyd, John   Survey   20 Sept 1754
630 acres on Little Troublesome ; Giles Tillott, James Barnhill: SCC.
Entered 20 June 1753

Boyd, John, Jr.   Survey   24 Sept 1754
229 acres on north side North Fork of Haw R.; Gile Fillot, James Barnhill: CB.
Entered 18 May 1753

Acock, James   Warrant   24 Oct 1754
640 acres on a br. of Crabtree; begin on north side James Acock line.
Entered 24 Oct 1754 - In lieu of an Entry made in Arthur Cook's name 20 Jan 1753.
Deed 8 Jan 1761

Robinson, John   Warrant   26 Oct 1754
640 acres in forks of Deep R.; begin at Duncan Campbell's line.
Entered 26 Oct 1754
"mouth Deep R."
Surveyed 7ber 27:55
Deed 9 Jan 1761 (280 acres?)

Barnet, Hugh   Warrant   29 Oct 1754
300 acres on both sides Mayo Cr.; Begin about the Lick Br.
Entered 17 Nov 1752
Deed 27 July 1760

Parker, Richard   Warrant   29 Oct 1754
640 acres on west side New Hope near mouth of Beaver Cr.
Entered 29 Oct 1754
Surveyed 31 May 1755 for 334 acres
Deed 1 Aug 1760

Boyd, John   Survey   9 Nov 1754
483 acres on north side Reedy Fork of Haw R.; adj. Bazil Brashear; on both sides Brashears Cr.; Otho Brashear, Jesse Brashear: CB.
Entered 20 June 1753

Blackwood, William   Survey   11 Nov 1754
640 acres on both sides Brashears Cr. waters of Reedy Fork of Haw River; Robert Samuel Brashear, Jesse Brashear: SCC.

Brashear, Middleton   Survey   12 Nov 1754
256 acres on Reedy Fork of Haw; Jesse Brashear, Robert Brashear: SCC.

Husband, Herman   Warrant   14 Nov 1754
640 acres on south side Rocky R. formerly entered by Robert Lowe.
Entered 14 Nov 1754
Survveyed 22 Aug 1757
Deed 5 Aug 1758

Husband, Herman   Warrant   14 Nov 1754
640 acres on Pole Cat, an entry known by the claim of Duke Kimbrough, below William Reynolds.
Entered 14 Nov 1754
On reverse "Lost by Duke Kimbrough he having got a deed from this Office."
"To be removed on or between the head branches of Sandy Creek & Rocky river Claimed by Zack. Martin Senr."

Johnston, John   Survey   18 Nov 1754
382 acres on a branch of Mudlick Cr.; Jacob Youngblood, Wm Vestall: SCC.

Mills, William   Survey   27 Nov 1754
216 acres on Stoney Creek, waters of Haw R., joins John West; Alexander West, Wm Mills, Jr.: SCC
Entered 9 June 1752

Jackson, Isaac   Survey   11 Dec 1754

240 acres on both sides Forristers Cr. below James Taylor; William Combs, Thos. Jackson SCC
Entered 10 Oct 1752

Dennis, John   Survey   12 Dec 1754
507 acres on branches of Buck Quarter, waters of Enoe; joins Isaac Jackson; Wm Combs, Jacob Morlley: CB.

Anderson, James   Survey   24 Dec 1754
247 acres on head branches of Forrester Creek, on both sides of Hico Road to Orange Court House; John Wood, David Anderson: SCC.

Lackkie, Allexander   Survey   2 Jan 1755
256 acres; joins Moses Emry, Coll. Rutherford; Samuell Steward, Joseph Dunkin: SCC.

Churton, William   Warrant   22 Jan 1755
460 acres on both sides of Cobb's Cr. near the head; that runs into Hico waters of the Dan.
Entered 21 Jan 1755
Deed 1 July 1755

Reynolds, David   Warrant   27 Jan 1755
640 acres on both sides the path that leads from Nathaniel Reeds to Gabriel Freemans; waters of Deep R.
Entered 27 Jan 1755
Surveyed 1 May 1755 for 280 acres
Deed 8 Jan 1760 (or 61)

Hightower, Austin   Survey   6 Feb 1755
640 acres on both sides the South Fork of Marks Cr. of Newhope above John Price's land; John Price, Thos Durham: SCC
Entered 14 Jan 1754

Howlet, William   Warrant   26 Feb 1755
640 acres on a branch of Licks Cr. called Sizemore Fork including the Indian Field to begin about a quarter of a mile below the fork.
Entered 16 Dec 1754
Surveyed 15 Apr 1756 ("To Wm Scaife")

Jackson, James   Warrant   26 Feb 1755
640 acres on the Eno R. joins his father & Thomas Willy; includes Beaverley's Cabbin.
Entered 2 Oct 1754
Assigned to Isaac Jackson
Surveyed 13 June 1757
Deed 27 July 1760

Husband, Herman   Warrant   26 Feb 1755
640 acres; Including an improvement on or near the head of the Great Alamance that Hugh Forster took from Jacob Armfield
Entered 11 Dec 1754
Surveyed 17 July 1756
Returned(?) May 1757
Deed 5 Nov 1757

Jackson, William   Warrant   26 Feb 1755
640 acres on the waters of New Hope Begin below Cates Path that goes from Esq. Mitchell to Cain Cr.
Entered 16 Dec 1754
Deed 2 Aug 1760

Hobson, George   Warrant   26 Feb 1755
640 acres on middle fork of Rocky R. joins Edmd Bray's line, a survey made by Zach. Martin, that he bought of him.
Entered 6 Jan 1755
Surveyed 6 Apr 1756
Deed 2 Aug 1760

Younger, James   Warrant   26 Feb 1755
640 acres on south side of Haw R. on both sides Brooks Cr. called Daves's Folly; includes Wm Marshes improvements.
Entered 19 Dec 1754
Assigned to William Marsh "living on the land"
Surveyed 30 Mar 1756

Morgan, Mark   Warrant   26 Feb 1755
640 acres on both sides Cubb Cr.
Entered 16 Dec 1754
Surveyed 11 Oct 1755
Deed 4 Nov 1756

Morgan, Mark   Warrant   26 Feb 1755
640 acres on both sides the northwest br. of New Hope; joins his former line to Robert Patterson.
Entered 11 Oct 1755
Deed 4 Nov 1756

McKinsey, Andrew   Warrant   26 Feb 1755
640 acres on a br. of Cain Cr. on the south side; joins Wm Helmes; includes Jos. Wright's improvements.
Entered 25 Dec 1754
Surveyed 11 May 1756
Deed 1 Aug 1759

Rhodes, Christopher   Warrant   26 Feb 1755
640 acres on a fk. of the North East prong of New Hope; joins Beasley & his own line.
Entered 6 Jan 1755
Deed 4 Nov 1756

Reed, Robert   Warrant   26 Feb 1755
400 acres on waters of New Hope at the head of
Lick Br.; joins Justice Patterson's plantation.
Entered 2 Sept 1754
Surveyed 22 Mar 1756
Deed 15 Mar 1759

Bird, John   Warrant   26 Feb 1755
640 acres on north side the South Fk. of Flatt R.
near the head of the Low Ground Br. - includes
Thos. Cate's improvements.
Entered 6 Jan 1755
"To Jno Pyson"
Assignment by Bird to Francis Bucknall 16 Nov
1756, wit: Thomas "B" Bucknall & Sarah "+" Bucknall.
Assignment by Francis Bucknall to Lawrence Redman
11 Aug 1759, wit: Richard Holman.
Assignment from Lawrence Redman to Jno Pyson 29
Jan 1761.

Pickett, William   Warrant   26 Feb 1755
640 acres on both sides Parkers Br. of New Hope;
joins Richd Parker, Valentine Braswell.
Entered 4 Nov 1754
Surveyed 2 June 1755
Deed 24 July 1760

Patterson, John, Esq.   Warrant   26 Feb 1755
640 acres; joins Richard Caswell's survey; includes a branch of Old Field Cr.
Entered 30 Sept 1754
Surveyed 17 June 1756
Deed 23 May 1758

Patterson, John, Esq.   Warrant   26 Feb 1755
640 acres on a branch of Lick Cr. below the Three
Springs.
Entered 16 Dec 1754
Surveyed 16 June 1756
Deed 20 May 1758

Murray, Benja   Warrant   26 Feb 1755
640 acres on head branches of Flatt R. & on the
Richland Mountain about a mile from Daniel Weldon.
Entered 4(?) Dec 1754
Deed 17 July 1760

Rhodes, John   Warrant   26 Feb 1755
640 acres on branches of Eno R.; joins Jas. Forrester; includes the Great Meadow.
Entered 28 Dec 1754
Assigned to William Rhodes
Deed 9 Feb 1761

Searcy, William   Warrant   26 Feb 1755
640 acres on both sides Deep R. to include Morgan
Nicks improvements & mouth of Fork Cr.
Entered 12 Dec 1754
Deed 7 Jan 1761

Searcy, William   Warrant   26 Feb 1755
640 acres joins his other entry.
Entered 12 Dec 1754
Surveyed 1 May 1756
Deed 2 Aug 1760

Ellison, John   Warrant   26 Feb 1755
640 acres on both sides Quarrels Cr. on west side
Flatt R.
Surveyed 2 Sept 1756 - To Archalaus Wilson
Deed 3 Feb 1761

Church, Thomas   Warrant   26 Feb 1755
640 acres on Fishing Cr., running up the North
Fork of Haw R.; includes his own improvements.
Entered 1 Jan 1755
Surveyed 8 Nov 1755
Deed 2 Aug 1760

McCullem, Henry   Warrant   26 Feb 1755
640 acres; Joins Thomas Wilkinson on Mountain Cr.
waters of Flatt R.
Entered 9 Dec 1754
Apparently transferrred to W. Combs

Harlan, Aaron   Warrant   26 Feb 1755
640 acres on both sides of Bigg Cr., alias Mountain Cr. - includes William Johnston's improvements; "running into Rocky River about 4 miles."
Entered 4 Nov 1754
"Harlans Creek"
Surveyed 1 Apr 1756
Deed 2 Aug 1760

Brashear, Robert   Warrant   26 Feb 1755
640 acres on both sides of Buffalo Cr. between
Brazil Brashear and Blackwood.
Entered 30 Dec 1754
Surveyed for Jesse Brashear 5 Sept 1755
Deed 17 July 1760

Creage, William   Warrant   26 Feb 1755
640 acres; Near head of New Cr., joins on the west
of his own line.
Entered 1 Oct 1754
Deed 20 Feb 1756

Blackson, William   Warrant   26 Feb 1755
640 acres on north side of Cain Cr., on Piney Br.;

joins "Valentine Hollinsworth that he bought of Zach. Martin, Senr.
Entered 6 Jan 1755
Surveyed 15 Nov 1756
Deed 9 Jan 1761

Bohannon, John   Warrant   26 Feb 1755
640 acres on 2nd fork of New Hope Cr.; joins John Rhodes (lowere tract).
Entered 26 Dec 1754
Surveyed 27 May 1755
Deed 2 Aug 1760

Nelson, Abram   Warrant   26 Feb 1755
640 acres on both sides Neuse R.; near mouth of Great Lick Cr.
Entered 30 Dec 1754
Surveyed 18 May 1756 for 350 acres.

Nelson, David   Warrant   26 Feb 1755
640 acres on branches of Andw Mitchell's Cr., waters of New Hope; above Mitchell's plantation.
Entered 7 Dec 1754
Surveyed 10 Aug 1757
Deed 22 Aug 1759
"To William Long"

Brooks, John   Warrant   26 Feb 1755
640 acres on south side Rocky R.; near head of Ephriam's Br.
Entered 6 Dec 1754
Surveyed 15 Apr 1756

Jones, John   Warrant   26 Feb 1755
640 acres on head branches of South & Middle Fork of Rocky R.; about 1 mile from James Alexander's.
Entered 26 Nov 1754
"no land removed Lying on the northeast side of Deep River in the fork or at the fork of Cedar Cr. - 10 June 1755"
Assigned to Danl Norris 10 Dec 1755
Surveyed 17 Apr 1756
Deed 10 May 1757

Mattock, Joseph   Warrant   26 Feb 1755
640 acres on both sides Eno R.; between Mr. Dickie & Henry Lemon above the old Trading Path.
Entered 12 Dec 1754
Surveyed 11 Sept 1756
Deed 22 Feb 1759

Linley, Thomas, Senr.   Warrant   26 Feb 1755
640 acres on southeast side Cain Cr., east side of Haw R.; on tract that goes out of Mitchel's Path to John Gray.
Deed 13 Nov 1756

Lewis, Enoch   Warrant   26 Feb 1755
640 acres on both sides Lick Cr.; includes Ephriam Seizmore's improvements.
Entered 30 Sept 1754
Surveyed 9 May 1755
Deed 10 May 1757

Martin, William   Warrant   26 Feb 1755
640 acres on east side Haw R., north side Cain Cr.; includes Zach. Martin's, John Harmon's & Eliz. Harding's improvements.
Entered 11 Dec 1754
"no land found" (interlined)
"old pattent"
"Removed to his own improvmt."
Surveyed 30 Mar 1756 for 187 acres
Deed 2 Aug 1760

Jones, Francis   Warrant   26 Feb 1755
640 acres on north side Cain Cr.; joins Hugh Laughlin & Thos Linley.
Entered 16 Dec 1754
"Removed ye South Side Deep River" (interlined)
"Ordered to Bear Creek"
Deed 22 Feb 1759
"May 13 1755 Francis Jones removes his warrant Lost by an Older Warrt of Hollingsworth lying in Orange County on Bear Creek about 3 or 4 miles above old Norris's"
Surveyed 8 June 1758

Bohannon, John   Warrant   26 Feb 1755
640 acres on 2nd fork of New Hope; upper survey.
Entered 26 Dec 1754
Surveyed (Probably) 27 May 1755
Deed 2 Aug 1760

Owen, Richd   Warrant   26 Feb 1755
640 acres on both sides Cain Cr.; about 1 1/4 miles above Capt. Cates.
Entered 4 Jan 1755
Assigned to Robert Cate
Surveyed for 560 acres 22 Sept 1756
Deed 5 Aug 1760

Holden, Thomas   Warrant   26 Feb 1755
640 acres on Buck Quarter, joins Capt. Synnot line on the south side.
Entered 9 Jan 1755
Surveyed 20 7br 1757
Deed 22 Aug 1759

Pryor, John   Warrant   27 Feb 1755
    640 acres on lower side of Ralph Griffin; on head
    of Aaron's Cr. & head of Grassy Cr.
    Entered 6 June 1753
    Deed 6 May 1757

Bracher, John   Warrant   27 Feb 1755
    640 acres above the mouth of Rushe branch on
    South Hico.
    Entered 14 May 1753
    Deed 2 Aug 1760

Maxwell, John   Warrant   27 Feb 1755
    640 acres on north side of Middle Br. of Dobbins
    Br. taking both sides of the south fork. (Dan
    River)
    Entered 6 Feb 1754
    "To be surveyed for William Bustar"
    Deed 2 Aug 1760

Barnet, Samuel   Warrant   27 Feb 1755
    640 acres 4 rods above McFarlin's Path on Gents
    Creek.
    Entered 6 Feb 1754
    Surveyed 8 April 1755
    Deed 25 July 1760

Barnett, Hugh   Warrant   27 Feb 1755
    640 acres; Beg, near Adam's Cr. below a New Cart
    Road.
    Entered 24 June 1754
    Surveyed 11 Apr 1755
    Assigned to James Curria
    Deed 15 July 1760

Dobbins, Hugh   Warrant   27 Feb 1755
    640 acres; Begin below a great spring near the
    fork of Cain Cr.
    Entered 10 May 1754
    (To n. Hico adjoining his other survey)
    Deed (?) 2 Aug 1760

Hughes, John   Warrant   27 Feb 1755
    640 acres On Hughs's Cr. below his mill; up north
    side of cr.
    Entered 26 Oct 1753
    Assigned to William Chambers 7 Apr 1755 - signed
    John "I" Hughs - Enoch Lewis, wit.
    Surveyed 7 Apr 1755
    Deed 17 July 1760

Laxton, Thomas   Warrant   27 Feb 1755
    640 acres; begin on Wm Chambers junr. line on
    Marlon Cr.
    Entered 5 June 1753
    Surveyed 13 Nov 1755
    Deed 7 July 1760

Hollingsworth, Valentine   Warrant   15 Mar 1755
    640 acres on west side Haw R. on forks of Cane
    Cr.; includes the place he & Henry Holliday now
    lives on.
    Entered 15 Mar 1755
    Surveyed 7 May 1756
    Deed 2 Aug 1760

Husband, Herman   Warrant   15 Mar 1755
    640 acres on or between the head branches of Sandy
    Cr. & Rocky R. being claimed by Zachariah Martin
    Senr.
    Entered 15 Mar 1755 "In Lieu of an Entry made 14
    Nov 1754"
    Surveyed 5 Oct 1756
    Deed 5 Aug 1758

Husband, Herman   Warrant   15 Mar 1755
    640 acres on the head of a branch of Sandy Cr.
    called Mount Pleasant on the east side of Deep R.
    including a cabin built by Soloman Allred &
    claimed by Zach. Martin.
    Entered 15 Mar 1755 "In Lieu of an Entry made the
    14 Nov 1754"
    Surveyed 2 May 1755

Aldrige. William   Warrant   15 Mar 1755
    640 acres on Mount Pleasant Run, a br. of Sandy
    Creek, Running into Deep River, the east side,
    Begin on the north end of a division line between
    him & Luke Smith.
    Entered 15 Mar 1755

Allrid, John   Warrant   15 Mar 1755
    640 acres on east side Deep R., on mouth of Mount
    Pleasant Run of Sandy Run; includes his and Thomas
    Alldrid's improvements; heretofore entered by John
    McDaniel.
    Entered 15 Mar 1755
    Surveyeed 2 May 1755
    Deed 15 Mar 1756

Branson, Thomas   Warrant   15 Mar 1755
    640 acres on Middle Br. of Rocky R.; joins his own
    land.
    Entered 15 Mar 1755
    Assigned to Richd Henderson
    Surveyed 5 May 1755

Cheney, James   Warrant   15 Mar 1755
    640 acres on west side Deep R., on Rich Land Cr.
    where Crafords Road crosses, being the place where

he now lives.
Entered 15 Mar 1755
Deed 26 Oct 1759

Chambers, William   Survey   7 Apr 1755
280 acres on Hughs's Mill Cr.; Luke Armsby, Saml Hughs: SCC.
Entered 26 Oct 1753

Barnet, Samuel   Survey   8 Apr 1755
250 acres on Fents Creek; joins William Barnet; Humphrey Barnet, Jesse Barnet: SCC.

Barnet, Hugh   Survey   11 Apr 1755
200 acres on Adams Cr.; Wm Guthrie, Robt Mitchell: SCC.
Entered 24 June 1754

Reynolds, David   Survey   1 May 1755
280 acres on branches of Polecat Cr., waters of Deep R.; both sides of path from Gab: Freeman to Nathl Reed; Wm Reynold, Jereh Reynold: SCC.

Howard, Stephen   Warrant   15 May 1755
350 acres on north side Deep R. opposite to Turnagain Point. "NB a former Entry made with Mr. Moseley."
Entered 14 May 1755
Surveyed 19 AApr 1756
Deed 10 May 1757

Powell, Nathaniel   Warrant   15 May 1755
400 acres at mouth of Indian Cr. of Deep R.
Entered 14 May 1755
"N:B: a former Entry made with Mr. Moseley"
Deed 5 Aug 1760

Ward, William   Warrant   15 May 1755
640 acres on east fk. of Sandy Cr.; includes improvements where he now lives.
Entered 15 May 1755
Surveyed - No date given

Carruthers, Joseph   Warrant   15 May 1755
400 acres on both sides Deep River joining Earl Granville's line being the place where the path crosses the river.
Entered 15 May 1755
Surveyed for 456 acres
Deed Jan 1758

Campbel, John   Warrant   16 May 1755
640 acres; Begin below William Armstrong on Moons Cr.

Entered 29 Jan 1755
Removed to Cobb's Cr.
Surveyed 22 Aug 1755
Deed 5 Nov 1756

Hart, David   Warrant   16 May 1755
640 acres on Lewis upper line on Wolfland Cr.
Entered 7 Dec 1754
Assigned to John Smith
Surveyed 17 Nov 1759

Husband, Herman   Warrant   16 May 1755
640 acres on Deep R. above the Targetts Rock opposite to the place called the Pocket.
Entered 13 May 1755
Surveyed 21 Apr 1756 (For 192 acres)
Deed 7 Nov 1757

Lane, Joseph   Warrant   16 May 1755
640 acres on both sides Swift Cr.; includes Days(?) improvements.
Entered 14 May 1755
"Wm Lane's name - Heir at Law
Deed 2 July 1760

Kilgore, Robert   Warrant   16 May 1755
640 acres on west corner of his own land; Hico Cr.
Entered 24 Jan 1755
Deed 2 Aug 1760

Husband, Herman   Warrant   16 May 1755
640 acres on Deep R. "a noted place well known by the name of the Pocket."
Entered 13 May 1755
Surveyed 19 Apr 1756 (For 540 acres)
Deed 7 Oct 1757

Cox's, Thos   Warrant   16 May 1755
40 acres on east side Richland Cr. of Deep R.; upon a run coming from the Pilot Mountain.
Entered 13 May 1755
Surveyed 28 Apr 1756
Deed 5 Aug 1758

Cox's Willm   Warrant   16 May 1755
640 acres on both sides Deep R. joins between his own two tracts on the west side of the R. and Peter Youngblood on the E. side of the R.
Entered 13 May 1755
Surveyed 4 May 1756
Deed 5 May 1757

Harris, Thomson   Warrant   16 May 1755
640 acres on the upper end of his own entry on

North fork of Hogans Cr.
Entered 18 Nov 1754
Surveyed 30 Aug 1755

Harris, Thomson   Warrant   16 May 1755
640 acres on south side Pruitts Fork.
Entered 18 Nov 1754
Surveyed 30 Aug 1755

Dobbin, Hugh   Warrant   16 May 1755
640 acres above McMillan on Hogan Cr.; includes the four Mile Lick.
Entered 24 Dec 1754
"To be in the name of Thos. Flaxon on Country Line Creek - Begin on Jos Dolittle's upper line - Wm Churton 12 June 1759"
"Executed (surveyed) for Saxon" - 381 acres

Kelly, John   Warrant   16 May 1755
640 acres; Begin at a pine near one of the sou(torn)rastes of the Double Creek thence running up between Double Creek & Hughes branch on the ridge including my two hundred acres.
Entered 7 Dec 1754
Deed 31 Jan 1761
"The plane to be returned in the name of James Anderson."

Harris, Thomson   Warrant   16 May 1755
640 acres; begin at North Fork of Hoggans Cr. called Pruit Fork at a red oak marked JW.
Entered 23 Jan 1755
Surveyed 28 Nov 1755
Deed 9 Jan 176(Torn)

Bohannon, John   Survey   27 May 1755
640 acres on 2nd fork of New Hope; adj. H. Patterson, Rhoades; Wm Rhodes, Christopher Rhodes: CB.
Entered 26 Dec 1754

Bohannon, John   Survey   27 May 1755
637 acres on 2nd fork of New Hope; William Rhoads, Christopher Rhoads: CB; Upper Survey.
Entered 26 Dec 1754

Parker, Richard   Survey   31 May 1755
334 acres on Lick Br. waters of New Hope; joins Robt. Hines; Robert Patterson, William Pickett: SCC.
Entered 29 Oct 1754.

Pickett, William   Survey   2 June 1755
456 acres; joins Parker, Braswell, Bear Tree Cr., Lick Br.; Richd Parker, Robert Patterson: SCC.
Entered 4 Nov 1754

Kain, Daniel   Survey   18 June 1755
575 acres on both sides Forrester's Cr.; Wm Combs, Geo. Dowther: SCC.

Harris, Thomson   Survey   30 Aug 1755
420 acres on Pruitts Fork waters of Hogans Cr.; joins his own line; John McCullom, Benja Knowls: SCC.
Entered 23 Jan 1755

Harris, Thomson   Survey   30 Aug 1755
420 acres on Pruitt Fork, waters of Hoggans Cr.; joins his lower survey; John McCullom, Benja Knowles: SCC.

Harris, Thomson   Survey   30 Aug 1755
405 acres on Pruitts Fork; John McCullom, Benjan Knowls: SCC.
Entered 18 Nov 1754

King, Peter   Survey   1 Sept 1755
560 acres on Little Troublesome & branches of Pruets Fork; Benajah King, Bethel Lively: SCC.
Entered 5 Mar 1752

Barshear, Jesse   Survey   5 Sept 1755
637 acres on Buffelo Cr.; Robt. Barshear, Robert Barshear, Junr: SCC.

Cate, Thos. Jr.   Survey   24 Sept 1755
556 acres on a fork of Cane Cr.; Thos Cate, Sr., Joseph Cate: SCC.

Robinson, John   Survey   27 Sept 1755
280 acres on Deep R.; adjoins Duncan Campbell's supposed line; Thomas Lantrum, Richard Barnet: SCC.
Entered 26 Oct 1754

Acock, James   Survey   1 Oct 1755
595 acres on head branches of Crabtree; adjoins Caswel's or Young's line; Arthur Cook, Joseph Lane, Jr.: CB.

Logue, John   Survey   6 Oct 1755
280 acres on head of the west fork of Eno R.; adjoins the late Gov. Johnston's line; James Lawford, Robert Anderson: SCC.

Boyd, John, Jr.   Survey   10 Oct 1755
424 acres on Great Troublesome begin in ye low grounds of ye creek in Churton's line; Marshal Lovelatty, Wm Kennidy: SCC.
Entered 23 May 1752

Morris, Henry   Survey   16 Oct 1755
 633 acres on head of Marks Cr. waters of New Hope on Harrys Mountain; Thomas Lloyd, Joshua Stroud: SCC.
 Entered 14 May 1753

Ballenger, Henry   Warrant   6 Nov 1755
 640 acres; Orange & Rowan Counties; on Alamance up a br. of Beaver Cr.; known by name of Ballinger's Land.
 Entered 6 Nov 1755
 Deed "In Jno Hanna name" 28 July 1760.

Church, Thomas   Survey   8 Nov 1755
 660 acres on Fishing Cr.; Begin at a hickory by the North Fork of Haw R.; Joseph Pinson, Edward Southwel: SCC.
 Entered 1 Jan 1755

Yarborough, Zachariah   Warrant   12 Nov 1755
 640 acres near mouth of Pocket Cr on north side Deep R.
 Entered 14 Oct 1755
 Surveyed for 280 acres
 Deed 3 Jan 1761

Tatum, Edward   Warrant   12 Nov 1755
 640 acres on both sides Bush Cr.; joins Benjamin Clements, John Hatley
 Entered 8 Sept 1755
 Surveyed 10 Sept 1756
 Assigned to Jas. Kerby
 Deed 7 Jan 1761

 Tatum, Edward - Bond from "Edward Tatum of Halifax County of Carolina" to James Kirby to make a title to "track" of land on both sides of Great Bush Cr. - Jno Falconer, John Kerby witnesses - no date

Lane, Jesse   Warrant   12 Nov 1755
 640 acres on both sides of White Oak Swamp; includes improvements of Chris. Edson.
 Entered 13 Oct 1755
 "The Land given to William Barker who bought the Improvements & leave to remove this warrant"

Haywood, Sherwood   Warrant   12 Nov 1755
 6340 acres on south side Dan R.; joins Mayo on Moon's Cr.
 Entered 7 Nov 1757
 Deed 26 Jan 1758
 On outside - "to be in John Armstrong")

Laxon, Thomas   Survey   13 Nov 1755
 640 acres on Marlers Cr.; Wm Chambers Junr., Wm Taylor: SCC.
 Entered 5 June 1753

Cox, Benjamin   Warrant   14 Nov 1755
 640 acres on Rich Land Cr. running into Deep R. on the west side of the r. being known by the name of Stoke's land.
 Entered 14 Nov 1755
 Surveyed (28 Apr 1756 interlined) 10 Oct 1759
 "To Nicholas Wireman Lost by Stokes"
 Deed 2 Aug 1760.

Dobbin, Hugh   Survey   19 Nov 1755
 408 acres on Both sides No Fork of North Hico; John Fairgison, Robt. Kilgore: SCC.

Harris, Thompson   Survey   28 Nov 1755
 420 acres on Pruits Fork waters of Hogans Cr.; Michael Joyce, George Vaughan: SCC.

Williams, William   Survey   6 Dec 1755
 640 acres on both sides Williams Cr.; "Begin at a white oak on the south side of Phillips Cr." Jese Lane, Thomas Davis: CB.
 Deed 4 Feb 1761

Dickson, Henry   Survey   7 Dec 1755
 330 acres on both sides Jint's(?) Cr. adjoining Barnet's line; Robert Dickson, Henry Dickson: SCC.

Lane, Joseph   Survey   8 Dec 1755
 360 acres; part in Johnston & part in Orange; joins Joseph Lane, Swift Creek; Henry Day, Thos Davis: SCC.
 Entered 14 May 1755

Carter, Finch   Warrant   3 Jan 1756
 640 acres adj. Samuel Sinat. on Hico Cr.
 Entered 4 Oct 1755
 Surveyed 5 Nov 1760
 Deed 29 Jan 1761

Stubbs, John   Warrant   24 Jan 1756
 640 acres on east br. of Brush Cr.; includes a birch tree marked IS.
 Entered 22 May 1755
 Deed 6 Nov 1756

York, Simon   Warrant   3 Feb 1756
 640 acres on both sides Sandy Cr., Deep R.
 Entered 9 Sept 1755
 "N:B: It should be Seymore York"
 Surveyed 7 May 1756
 Deed 5 Aug 1758

Hopkins, John   Warrant   3 Feb 1756

300 acres on north side Deep R. about a mile below Soloman Aldridge's; includes William Croddin's improvements.
Entered 29 Oct 1755
Surveyed 5 Nov 1756

Emory, John   Warrant   3 Feb 1756
640 acres on south fork of Little R.; joins the late Gov. Johnston's line, now bought by Alexander Mebane.
Entered 10 Dec 1755
Assigned to Alexander Torintine
Deed 9 Feb 1761

Vestall, William   Warrant   3 Feb 1756
400 acres on North Fork of Rocky R.; where he lives.
Entered 7 July 1755
Surveyed 6 Apr 1756
Deed 9 Nov 1757

Strauhon, Gilbert   Warrant   3 Feb 1756
400 acres on east fork of Sandy Cr; joins Herman Husband; includes John Wiris improvements.
Entered 6 Oct 1756
Surveyed 9 June 1757

Temple, Samuel   Warrant   3 Feb 1756
640 acres on both sides Bear Cr. of Haw R.; about a mile below Cape Fear Rd.; lying over against head of George's Cr. & against head of Horse Br.
Entered 9 Sept 1755
Surveyed 17 Apr 1756 for 223 acres
Deed 1 Mar 1759

Morrow, William   Warrant   3 Feb 1756
640 acres on waters of Cain Cr.; including 3 improvements of William Mears.
Entered 10 Oct 1755
Surveyed 10 May 1756
Deed 23 May 1758 for 552 acres

Beal, John   Warrant   3 Feb 1756
640 acres on south side Deep R., on Mendenhall Cr.; near the mouth; begin near the lower Fall; (Orange or Rowan).
Entered 10 July 1755
Surveyed for 238 acres
Deed 3 Aug 1760

Bohannon, Duncan   Warrant   3 Feb 1756
A re-survey on his own & James Trice's land; Deed granted by Colo. Corbin & Innes & all vacant land adjoining above the mouth of a fork of the Great Lick (New Hope Cr.)

Entered 9 Sept 1755
Surveyed 22 June 1756
Deed 3 Jan 1761

Martin, Peter   Warrant   3 Feb 1756
640 acres on Panthers Cr. waters of New Hope; includes his improvements.
Entered 16 June 1755
Surveyed 27 May 1756 for 630 acres
Deed 3 Jan 1761

Mitchell, Andrew, Esq.   Warrant   3 Feb 1756
300 acres on waters of New Hope; begin where Joseph Mattock got his Mill Stones on the path that leads from Orange Court House to the said Mitchell's plantation.
Entered 10 Oct 1755
Surveyed 14 Oct 1757
Deed 1756(?)

Lindley, Thomas   Warrant   3 Feb 1756
640 acres on south prong of Cain Cr. at a place called Fisher's Place formerly surveyd for Zachariah Martin Senr.
Entered 26 June 1755.
Surveyed 8 May 1756.
Deed 22 Feb 1759.

Bohannon, John   Warrant   3 Feb 1756
640 acres on the north east br. of New Hope; joins his own line that he bought of Henry Beasley.
Entered 9 Dec 1755
Assigned to Benjamn. Saxon
Deed (Possibly 12 Feb 1761)

Reed, William   Warrant   3 Feb 1756
640 acres on both sides Deep R.; begin below the mouth of RichLand Cr., called the Haw Fields, include the good land & low ground on both sides the river to Crooked Cr. - includes Josiah Wallace's improvements.
Entered 13 Dec 1755
Surveyed 6 Nov 1756
Deed 2 Aug 1760

Allen, Morrell   Warrant   3 Feb 1756
640 acres on a south branch of Cain Cr.; joins Fisher's line.
Entered 10 Oct 1755
"Entry not paid, W.C."
"Allen to John Pile"

Wiley, William   Warrant   3 Feb 1756
640 acres on Birch Cr. running into the north fk. of Little Alamance, running up the sd. Birch Cr.

to and across the Quaker Rd.
Entered 10 June 1755
Surveyed 13 Aug 1756 for 636 acres

Wiley, Hugh   Warrant   3 Feb 1756
640 acres on Beaver Cr. waters of Little Alamance; joins Henry Ballinger.
Entered 10 June 1755
Surveyed 2 Nov 1756

Wagner, Henry   Warrant   3 Feb 1756
400 acres on Tapley's Cr.; joins land where McCarver did live.
Entered 9 Sept 1755
Surveyed 6 Sept 1756
Deed 18 July 1760

Rhoads, Hezekiah   Warrant   3 Feb 1756
640 acres on both sides the third fork of New Hope Cr.; begin just above the Great Lick. Includes Phileman Munchy's Cabbin.
Entered 5 June 1755
Surveyed 21 June 1756 for 472 acres.

Stroud, John, Junior Warrant   3 Feb 1756
640 acres on Collins Cr.; joins William Meban's upper line.
Entered 23 May 1755
Surveyed 13 Aug 1757

Stroud, John   Warrant   3 Feb 1756
640 acres on waters of New Hope; begin just above Lloyd's Path; includes his own improvements.
Entered 13 Oct 1755
Surveyed 23 Sept 1756
Deed 25 July 1760

Cox, William, Senior Warrant   3 Feb 1756
640 acres; In trust for Samuel Allen Orphan; on both sides Cox's Cr.; joins Cox's upper line and on the east side of Deep R.
Entered 1 Nov 1755
Surveyed 29 Apr 1756

Day, Mary   Warrant   3 Feb 1756
640 acres on both sides a prong of Cain Cr. about a mile above Thomas Cate's Place.
Entered 20 Sept 1755
Surveyed 11 Aug 1757
Deed 9 Feb 1761

Fields, Jane   Warrant   3 Feb 1756
640 acres on the head branches of the Great Alamance, about two miles north of Mr. McGee, including his own improvements.

Entered 3 Nov 1753(5?)
Surveyed 19 Aug 1757
Deed 25 July 1760

Nicks, John   Warrant   3 Feb 1756
640 acres; joins Thomas Dannall; the land he now lives on; on North side Buffelo Cr; east side of Dannall.
Entered 12 June 1755
Assigned to Thomas Hamilton
Surveyed 10 July 1756

Erwin, Robert   Warrant   3 Feb 1756
300 acres on west side of Enoe on both sides the Great Road that goes to the old Court House and upper ford of Haw R.; about a mile from the Enoe.
Entered 9 Dec 1755
Deed 2 May 1760

Bellwin, Robert   Warrant   3 Feb 1756
640 acres on south side of Neuse R. on branches of Great Lick Creek & Laurel Creek; between Osborn Jeffreies two tracts.
Entered 9 Dec 1755
Deed 8 Jan 1761

Carson, Alexander   Warrant   3 Feb 1756
500 acres on both sides the Enoe below Isaac Jackson's called the Rich Bottom.
Entered 10 Dec 1755
Surveyed 6 Sept 1756
Deed 15 July 1760

Powell, Lucas   Warrant   3 Feb 1756
640 acres on both sides of the watery Fork of Cain Cr.
Entered 10 June 1755
Assigned to Sackfield Brewer
Surveyed 12 Aug 1757
Deed 3 Aug 1760

Mabry, Francis   Warrant   3 Feb 1756
640 acres on both sides Buffelo Cr.; joins Brogden on south side of Tarr R.
Entered 3 Jan 1756
Deed 11 May 1757

McNight, John   Warrant   3 Feb 1756
640 acres on north side of N. Buffalo Cr., a br. of Haw R.; formerly surveyed by James Carter for the said Night but no Entry to be found.
Entered 26 June 1755
Surveyed 9 July 1756
Deed 22 Aug 1759

Howlett, William   Warrant   3 Feb 1756
    640 acres on north side Haw R.; opposite to Cain Cr.; includes Hezekiah Collins' improvements.
    Entered 26 June 1755
    Surveyed 9 Apr 1756
    Deed 1 Jan 1761

Rhodes, Christopher   Warrant   3 Feb 1756
    640 acres on Crooked Cr., a br. of New Hope; below Robert Patterson.
    Entered 17 June 1755
    Surveyed for 593 acres
    Deed 29 July 1760

Swansey, Henry   Warrant   3 Feb 1756
    640 acres; adjoins entry of Daniel Williams; Cain Cr., Haw R.
    Assigned to William Lee - 16 Nov 1756
    Returned for 375 acres.
    Deed 1 Aug 1760

Williams, Daniel   Warrant   3 Feb 1756
    640 acres on Lick Br. on south side Cain Cr.; known as Noll's Entry.
    Entered 20 Nov 1755
    Assigned to James Lindley - 16 Nov 1756
    Returned for 240 acres
    Deed 2 Aug 1760

McKey, Anne   Warrant   3 Feb 1756
    300 acres on north fork of Little R.; joins his own, William Bogan's, John Dunnagan's & Joseph Ellison's lines.
    Entered 10 Dec 1755
    Surveyed 5 Dec 1757
    Deed 2 Aug 1760

Churton, William   Warrant   3 Feb 1756
    640 acres on Dutchman's Cr., waters of Eno; joins Col. Corbin.
    Entered 26 June 1755

Couch, William   Warrant   3 Feb 1756
    300 acres on the head of Rich Fork.
    Entered 23 Sept 1755
    Surveyed 9 June 1757
    Deed 28 July 1760

Miller, George   Warrant   3 Feb 1756
    320 acres on branches of Forister Cr., waters of Little R.
    Entered 11 Dec 1755
    Surveyed 22 Dec 1756
    Deed 15 July 1760

Gould, Ephriam   Warrant   27 Feb 1756
    640 acres on north side Crane Cr. between mouth of cr. & where Stewart's Path crosses cr.
    Entered 12 May 1753
    Surveyed 12 Apr 1756
    Deed 13 Nov 1756

Martin, John, Esq.   Survey   26 Mar 1756
    247 acres on Northeast Fork of New Hope waters, joins Moore's line; John Burt, Wm Blake: SCC.
    Entered 13 June 1754.

Martin, John   Survey   29 Mar 1756
    520 acres on both sides Brooks Cr. waters of Haw R.; Charles Foushee, John Marsh: SCC.

Martin, William   Survey   30 Mar 1756
    187 acres on south side Haw R.; Zachariah Martin, George Martin: SCC.
    Entered 11 Dec 1754.

Marsh, William   Survey   30 Mar 1756
    640 acres on south side Haw R. on Little Cr. & Brooks Cr., joins John Martin; John Stuart, William Marsh, Jr.: SCC
    Entered 19 Dec 1754.

Fooshe, Charles   Survey   31 Mar 1756
    640 acres on south side Haw R., both sides Robisons Cr.; Robert Marsh, Robert Pamplen: SCC.

Harlan, Aaron   Survey   1 Apr 1756
    536 acres on Harlans Cr. waters of Rocky R.; John Nethery, John Harvy: SCC.
    Entered 4 Nov 1754.

Barns, Brinsley   Survey   5 Apr 1756
    640 acres on both sides Rocky R. & mouth of Muddlick Cr.; James Barns, George Hobson, Jr.: CB

Hobson, George   Survey   6 Apr 1756
    240 acres on middle fork of Rocky R.; George Hobson, Junr., James Barns: SCC.
    Entered 6 Jan 1755

Hollinsworth, Valentine   Survey   7 Apr 1756
    420 acres on west side of Haw R. on the fork of Cane Cr., joins Hugh Laughlan, said Hollinsworth, Thos Lindley; Hugh Laughlan, Thomas Green: SCC.

Howlet, William   Survey   9 Apr 1756
    189 acres on north side Haw R.; John Bauldin, Joshua Morgan: SCC.
    Entered 26 June 1755

Scaife, William   Survey   15 Apr 1756
    264 acres on both sides Sizemores Br. the south
    side of Rocky R.; Thos. Brooks, John Brooks: SCC.

Yarborough, Zachariah   Survey   21 Apr 1756
    280 acres on north side Deep R.; joins Jesse Hol-
    lingsworth; Stephen Howard, Nathanl. Powel: SCC.
    Entered 14 Oct 1755.

Powell, Nathaniel   Survey   22 Apr 1756
    700 acres on north side Deep R., both sides Indian
    Cr., joins Stephen Howard; Stephen Howard, Thos.
    Smith: SCC.

Evans, Jacob   Survey   30 Apr 1756
    230 acres; joins Deep R. on the south side; David
    Brown, John Lawrence: SCC.
    Entered 26 Apr 1754

Searcy, William   Survey   1 May 1756
    640 acres on both sides Deep R., joins his land;
    Wm Reed, John Burd: SCC.
    Entered 12 Dec 1754

Searcy, William   Survey   1 May 1756
    640 acres on both sides Deep R.; Wm Reed, John
    Burd: CB.
    On reverse - "Warrt lost or mislaid"

Husband, Herman   Survey   5 May 1756
    641 acres on both sides Sandy Cr., joins Samuel
    Walker, Thos Branson; Saml Walker, John Guston:
    SCC.
    Entered 14 Nov 1754

Hill, Thomas   Warrant   6 May 1756
    640 acres; Begin just below the mouth of Rocky R.
    & on N. side of Deep R.
    Entered 6 May 1756
    Deed 2 Aug 1760

Robinson, William   Warrant   6 May 1756
    640 acres on Reedy Fork of Haw R.
    Entered 6 May 1756
    Deed 10 June 1758

Steward, John   Warrant   6 May 1756
    640 acres on south side Haw R. on both sides
    Robinson's Cr., includes improvements John Steward
    bought of John Robinson, being the place where
    John Robinson was killed.
    Entered 6 May 1756
    Surveyed 3 Oct 1757

Pattterson, John   Warrant   6 May 1756
    140 acres on New Hope.
    Entered 6 May 1756
    Surveyed 25 Oct 1757
    Deed 23 May 1758

James, Thomas   Warrant   10 May 1756
    640 acres on north fork of Little R. below the
    mouth of Horse Creek.
    Entered 10 May 1756
    Deed 22 Jan 1761

Wooddy, John   Survey   12 May 1756
    374 acres on south side Haw R.; Thomas Lindley,
    Frances Jones: CB.

Usrey, William   Warrant   13 May 1756
    640 acres on Mayo Cr.
    Entered 11 Nov 1755
    "Surveyed by a old warrant for Hugh Barnet this
    to be removed by Wm Chambers"
    "to be removed the land taken by a older warrant"
    Joyning of Michl. Dickson's line and on the East
    side of Marlowe Cr. a branch of Hico - 640 acres.

Falconer, John   Warrant   13 May 1756
    640 acres on Great Bush Cr., adjoins John Hatley.
    Entered 9 Apr 1756
    Deed 10 Sept 1756

Lewis, Enoch   Warrant   13 May 1756
    640 acres on north side Deep R., opposite Zacha-
    riah Martin's survey where Gilbert Paterson now
    lives.
    Entered 5 May 1756
    Surveyed 10 Nov 1756
    Deed 11 May 1757

Hart, David   Warrant   16 May 1756
    640 acres; Begin at mouth of Lick Cr. on Moons
    Cr., up both sides Lick Fork.
    Entered 7 Dec 1754
    (David Hart - Removed) - "to be in name of Nicka-
    lis Hill"
    Deed 9 Jan 1761

Dobbins, Hugh   Warrant   16 May 1756
    640 acres above McMillan's on Hogans Cr., includes
    the four mile lick
    Entered 24 Dec 1754
    Surveyed for Thos. Laxon as 381 acres
    "To be in the name of Thos. Flaxon on Country Line
    Creek Begin on Jas Dolittle when done" signed Wm
    Churton

Harris, Thomson   Warrant   16 May 1756

640 acres on north fork Hogans Cr. called Pruitt Fork
Entered 23 Jan 1755
Surveyed 28 Nov 1755
Deed 9 Jan 176(torn)

Nelson, Abram   Survey   18 May 1756
350 acres (Orange or Johnston Co.) on both sides Neuse R. & mouth of Greaty Lick Cr.; Wm Reeves, Robt Belvin: SCC.

Belvin, Robert   Survey   19 May 1756
521 acres on Great Lick Cr. waters of Neuse, joins Capt. Jeffrey's; Abraham Nelson, Wm Goodson: SCC.
Entered 9 Dec 1755

Rhoads, Christopher   Survey   26 May 1756
593 acres on both sides Crooked Cr., waters of New Hope, joins Mark Morgan, Joseph Barby; Henry Beesley, Richard Hobson: CC.
Entered 11 June 1755

Martin, Peter   Survey   27 May 1756
630 acres on both sides of Panther Cr. a fork of North East of New Hope; Christopher Rhoads, Henry Beesly: SCC.
Entered 16 June 1755

Walker, John   Warrant   3 June 1756
450 acres on northeast side the Haw R. at a place called the Red Field; begin at a white oak on east side Poke Berry Cr., includes two plantations where he now lives & James Collin's.
Entered 17 June 1755
Surveyed 2 Apr 1756 (?)
Deed for 468 acres 23 May 1758

Rhodes, Issachar (Hezekiah) Survey   21 June 1756
472 acres on 3rd fork of New Hope Cr., joins Joseph Barby; George Hearn, Wm Watts: SCC.

Bohannon, Duncan, Jr. Survey   22 June 1756
205 acres on Newhope Cr., joins his own land; Edward Trice, Joseph Bohannon: SCC.
Entered 9 Sept 175_

Barnett, Hugh   Survey   22 June 1756
573 acres on both sides of Mayo Cr. begin on the Lick Br.; Edwd. Chambers, James Wilson: SCC.
Entered 27 Nov 1752

Hamilton, Thomas   Survey   10 July 1756
643 acres, "Surveyd for Thos Hamilton Between No(3) and Numbr(4) ye Irish tracts on North Buffelo"; In both Orange and Rowan Counties; joins Donnel; Hugh Brally, James Brown: SCC.

Beals, John   Survey   29 July 1756
238 acres on both sides Mendinghales Cr., below the lower falls, the south side Deep R.; John Mills, John Beals, Jr.: CB. (Survey lists as being in Rowan Co.)

Wiley, William   Survey   13 Aug 1756
636 acres on Birch Cr. waters of little Allamance & on both sides the Quaker Rd.; Peter Lehugh, Edward Self: SCC.
Entered 10 June 1755.

Wiley, William   Survey   16 Aug 1756
640 acres on both sides the north fk. of great Allamance & mouth of Birch Cr.; John McDaniel, Cornelius McDeade: SCC.
Entered 10 June 1755.

Wilson, Archelus   Survey   2 Sept 1756
283 acres on Quarrel Cr., joins Richard Holoman, Phileman Bradford; Richard Holoman, Charles Moore: SCC.
Deed 3 Feb 1761

Holeman, Richard   Survey   2 Sept 1756
384 acres on Quarrel Cr. waters of Flatt R., joins James Dickens, Bradford, Thos Bradford, Wade (or Weldon); Archelus Wilson, Charles Moore: SCC.
Entered 4 Mar 1754 (by Jas. Taylor)

Waggoner, Henry   Survey   3 Sept 1756
172 acres on Tapley's Cr., joins McCallister; Archalaus Wilson, George Wagoner: SCC.

Carson, Alexander   Survey   6 Sept 1756
108 acres on both sides of Enoe R.; Isaac Jackson, Robert Wilson: SCC.
Entered 10 Dec 1755

Tatum, Edward   Survey   10 Sept 1756
360 acres on Bush Cr., joins John Hatley; Sherrod Hatley, James Bynum: CC.

Falconer, John   Survey   10 Sept 1756
252 acres on Great Bush Cr., waters of New Hope; adjoins John Hatley; Sherod Hatley, James Bynum: CB.

James, Thomas   Survey   13 Sept 1756
487 acres on both sides Horse Creek, a branch of Little River; Thomas Parkings, Willm. Burney: SCC.

Cate, Robert   Survey   22 Sept 1756

560 acres on north side Haw R. opposite mouth of Ferrals Cr., adjoins James Collins; James Collins, John Dover: CB.

Stroud, John, Sr.   Survey   23 Sept 1756
240 acres on both sides New Hope Cr.; Joshua Eason, Joshua Stroud: SCC.
Entered 13 Oct 1755.

Bracher, John   Survey   27 Sept 1756
140 acres on both sides of South Hico Cr.; George Lea, Cornilas Dollerhide: SCC.

Anderson, James   Survey   27 Sept 1756
641 acres on branches of Doble Creek; Lewis Howell, John Huges: SCC.

Wiley, Hugh   Survey   2 Nov 1756
567 acres on Beaver Cr. waters of little Alamance, joins John McGowin, Joseph Davis, Cusick; John McGowin, Wm Davis: SCC.

McGowin, John   Survey   2 Nov 1756
628 acres in Orange & Rowan on both sides of Beaver Cr. waters of Allamance; Benja Starratt, Walter Matthews: SCC.
Entered 6 Nov 1755.

Hackoney, Lamuell   Receipt   4 Nov 1756
Rec. of Lamuell Hackony 5 shills for writing for Barnebe Godwin - Jno Haywood.

Hopkins, John   Survey   5 Nov 1756
200 acres on both sides Deep R.; Wm Allred, Lambeth Hopkins: SCC.
Deed 12 Jan 1761

Reed, William, Esq.   Survey   6 Nov 1756
480 acres on Deep R. & Brush Cr.; Thomas Graves, Richard Curtis: SCC.

Burt, John   Warrant   9 Nov 1756
640 acres on Stirrup Iron Cr., Brier Cr., adjoins Capt. Edward Jones, includes his improvements on north fork of Crabtree Cr.
Entered 9 Nov 1756
Deed 18 July 1760

Warrin, Henry   Warrant   9 Nov 1756
640 acres at or near land of Osburn Jefferys, on both sides Barton Cr.
Entered 25 June 1756
Deed 22 July 1761

Farguson, John   Warrant   11 Nov 1756
640 acres on both sides Reedy Fork of Hico, joins Hugh Dobbin.
Entered 14 Sept 1756
Deed 8 Nov 1757

Talbert, James   Warrant   11 Nov 1756
640 acres, begin at Capt. Banksones west corner.
Entered 27 Sept 1756
Deed 29 July 1760

Hill, Thomas   Survey   11 Nov 1756
110 acres on n. side Deep R. at mouth of Rocky R., Includes two small islands; Joseph Brantley, Lewis Brantley: SCC.
Entered 6 May 1756.

Walker, Samuel   Warrant   13 Nov 1756
640 acres on waters of Sandy Cr., where he lives.
Entered 13 Nov 1756
Surveyed 17 Aug 1757
Deed 22 Feb 1759

Braxon, William   Survey   15 Nov 1756
262 acres on south side Haw R. & Cane Cr. on Piney Br.; James Lindley, Henry Holliday: CB.

Lindley, James   Survey   16 Nov 1756
200 acres on Lick Br., waters of Terrils Cr.; Wm Braxon, John Boldin: CB.

Lee. William   Survey   16 Nov 1756
375 acres on lick br., waters of Ferrels Cr.; Wm Braxon, Henry Holiday: CB.
Entered 20 Nov 1755

Lindley, James   Survey   17 Nov 1756
330 acres on south side Haw R. & Cain Cr., joins Lambert, Howlett, James Lindley; John Baldin, Simon Lindley: SCC.

Bohannon, Duncan   Survey   21 Nov 1756
695 acres On Deep River at mouth of Rocky R.; Wm Murfey, Joseph Brantley: SCC.

Brashear, Robert   Survey   2 Dec 1756
640 acres on both sides of Reedy Fork of Haw, joins Robert Brashear, Bazil Brashear, on Buffalo; Bazil Brashear, John Hallum: SCC. (Entry originally in name of Edward Southwell)

Trollinger, Jacob Henry Survey   6 Dec 1756
160 acres on west side Haw R. & both sides the New Trading Path; Stophel Head, George Trout: SCC.

Miller, George   Survey   22 Dec 1756

270 acres on drains of Forister Cr., adjoins Robert Davis, Miller; Robert Davis, Robert Wilson: CB.

Roberson, Luke   Survey   28 Jan 1757
550 acres on south side Highco Cr., begin on County line at John Pryor's; Lawrence Rambo, John Murey: CB.
Entered 6 Oct 1755

Kilgore, Robert   Survey   2 Feb 1757
213 acres, joins his own land; John Roberson, John Daniel: SCC

McDaniel, John   Warrant   5 Feb 1757
640 acres on Sandy Cr., on his own place, on west side Haw River, near mouth of Alamance, provided it does not fall in McCulloch's line, on the Haw R. tract.
Entered 5 Feb 1757
"In lieu of McDaniell's Warrant, now in Churton's Hands, the land being granted to John Aldridge."

Runalds, Dudley   Survey   8 Feb 1757(?)
240 acres on both sides Moon's Cr.; Hugh Dobbins, John Ferguson: SCC.

Dobbin, Hugh   Survey   9 Feb 1757
532 acres on both sides Hogans Cr., joins Ferguson; Jno Ferguson, Hugh Taylor: SCC.

Hill, Nicholas   Survey   10 Feb 1757
360 acres on branches of Moon's Cr & Honiley's Cr.; Edmond Denney, Thomas Hughes: SCC.
Entered 7 Dec 1754 (by David Hart).

Hill, Nikolas   Survey   10 Feb 1757
360 acres on br. of Moons Cr. & Hawleys Cr.; Edmond Denny, Thomas Hughes: SCC.
Entered 7 Dec 1754
Deed 9 Jan 1761

Murrey, Benja   Survey   21 Feb 1757
180 acres on branches of Deep Cr.; James Satterfield, William Jay: SCC.
Entered 4 Dec 1754.

Winborne, William   Warrant   7 May 1757
640 acres, joins Herman Husbands land on Deep R.
Entered 7 May 1757
Surveyed 27 Sept 1757
Deed 9 Jan 1761.

Holles, Moses   Warrant   12 May 1757
640 acres on north side of Dan R. between Jas. Mayho & Alexr. Gowing.
Entered 26 Apr 1757
Deed 2 Jan 1761

Long, Benjamin   Warrant   12 May 1757
640 acres on both sides Storeys Cr., adjoins Lackston.
Entered 31 Jan 1757.
Deed 4 Mar 1761.

Bledsoe, Jacob   Warrant   12 May 1757
640 acres on both sides of Bartons Cr waters of Flat R., includes Obediah Terrell's improvements
Entered 14 Feb 1757
"To John Bledsoe - Removed - Surveyed"

Bird, Burgon   Warrant   12 May 1757
640 acres on both sides of a branch of Tarr R.
Entered 14 Jan 1757
Surveyed 24 July 1760
Deed 27 Jan 1761

Armstrong, William   Warrant   12 May 1757
640 acres, begin on Mayho's line on south side Dan R.
Surveyed for Alexr. Bollin.
Entered 5 May 1757
Surveyed 17 July 1760
Deed 31 Jan 1761

Roper, David   Warrant   12 May 1757
640 acres on Rattlesnake Cr.
Entrered 26 (Torn) 1757
Deed for 642 acres 23 July (Torn)

Morgan, Mark   Warrant   14 May 1757
640 acres joining his lower line & running down on both sides the Creek.
Entered 2 Nov 1756
Surveyed 14 Nov 1758

Morgan, Mark   Warrant   14 May 1757
640 acres, joins his lower line.
Entered 4 Nov 1756
Surveyed 14 Nov 1758

Morgan, Mark   Warrant   14 May 1757
640 acres on forks of New Hope called Main New Hope & Morgan's Cr.
Entered 4 Nov 1756
Surveyed 15 Nov 1758

Milton, Robert   Warrant   14 May 1757
640 acres on north side Haw R. below the red field at the Great Falls above the mouth of Second Br.

Entered 4 Nov 1756
"To Nathan Melton his heir"
Surveyd 25 Oct 1759
Deed 30 July 1760

Reed, William &   Warrant   14 May 1757
Churton, William
   640 acres on both sides the old courthouse road on the east side the River Eno, between the town & John Gray.
   Entered 27 Dec 1756

Morgan, Mark   Warrant   14 May 1757
   640 acres on New Hope Cr., joins his upper line & Mulkey.
   Entered 4 Nov 1756
   Surveyed 8 May 1758

Bowie, James   Warrant   14 May 1757
   640 acres on both sides of Ellybee's Cr. includes the Big Springs, adjoins Robt. Cromby's upper line.
   Entered 20 Dec 1756
   Assigned to Robert Clinton

Marsh, John   Warrant   14 May 1757
   640 acres on south side Haw R., both sides Little Creek, above Hercules Henderson, about 2 miles; against the Red Fields, includes his own & James Younger's improvements.
   Entered 14 Dec 1756
   Surveyed 7thber 30th 1757
   Deed 2 Aug 1761

Churton, William   Warrant   14 May 1757
   400 acres on head branches of Dutchman's Cr. and both sides a path that goes from the Town of Corbinton to Andrew Mitchell's where there was formerly an old cabin.
   Entered 20 May 1756
   Deed 31 Jan 1761

Fuller, James   Warrant   14 May 1757
   640 acres between Rocky R. & Deep R., near the fork.
   Entered 15 Dec 1756
   (N.B. Ye right name is Joseph Fuller)
   Surveyed 5 June 1758
   Deed 3 Feb 1761

Brashear, Robert Samuel   Warrant   14 May 1757
   640 acres in the fork of South & North Buffelo, adjoins Thomas Donald.
   Entered 15 Dec 1756
   Deed 8 Aug 1760

Culbertson, James   Warrant   14 May 1757
   640 acres on waters of Little R., joins south side of late Gov.'s line between No 23 & 28.
   Entered 15 Dec 1756
   Assigned to David Mitchel
   Surveyed 13 Nov 1757
   Deed 30 July 1760

Bohannon, Duncan   Warrant   14 May 1757
   640 acres on south side Deep R., joins county line, includes improvements of John Collins, Matthew Caps, joins Lord Granville's line.
   Entered 11 Oct 1756
   Deed 28 Feb 1761(?)

Baker, Andrew   Warrant   16 May 1757
   640 acres on Little Barton Cr. on south side Neuse R.
   Entered 9 Mar 1757
   Assigned to Nathaniel Kimbrough
   Surveyed 2 July 1757
   Deed 25 July 1760

Abecromby, Robt.   Warrant   16 May 1757
   320 acres on both sides Ellebees Cr., begin below the Lick.
   Entered 2 May 1756
   Surveyed 7 Dec 1757
   Deed 22 Feb 1759

Stubbs, Thomas   Warrant   16 May 1757
   640 acres on the head branches of Bigg Cr. waters of Enoe, joins William Combs, includes ye meeting house.
   Entered 5 Mar 1757
   Assigned to John Carson
   Surveyed 5 Dec 1757

Brown, David   Warrant   16 May 1757
   640 acres on waters of the Great Alamanchy on the north side on a branch known as Qualle Run where one Thos Landers thought of entering.
   Entered 5 July 1756
   Surveyed 24 Nov 1757
   Deed 7 Aug 1760

Brewer, Henry   Warrant   16 May 1757
   640 acres on fork of Ferrell's Cr. on north side of Haw, on both sides of Cape Fear Road.
   Entered 9 Mar 1757
   Surveyed 8 Oct 1757

Cantril, Jos.   Warrant   16 May 1757
   600 acres on both sides of Toms Cr. being the place where he now lives on the waters of Stoney

Cr. waters of Haw R.
Entered 8 June 1756
Surveyed 9 Nov 1757

Cargan, John   Warrant   16 May 1757
640 acres near the mouth of Spirit Br. between
Thos Willy & Hugh Wood on the south side of Enoe.
Entered 29 Sept 1756
Surveyed 22 July 1758
Deed 7 Aug 1760

Herndon, George   Warrant   16 May 1757
640 acres on both sides the NE fork of New Hope
about a half mile up the cr.
Entered 8 June 1756
Surveyed 13 Feb 17__

Frazier, John   Warrant   16 May 1757
640 acres lying between the two roads from the
town to the west on a path to Maddock's Mill.
Entered 8 Mar 1757
Surveyed 19 Dec 1759
Deed 30 July 1760

Moss, James   Warrant   16 May 1757
640 acres on waters of New Hope on north side,
includes his own improvements.
Entered 14 June 1756
Surveyed 31 Aug 1759
Assigned to William Cox
Deed 1 July 1760

Terrel, James   Warrant   16 May 1757
640 acres on the east & west line that former-
ly belonging to Giles Tillot on both sides Roses
Cr. a br. of Haw R. called the Beaver Dam Fk.
Entered 28 Feb 1757
"True Name is James Sterret"
Surveyed 17 Nov 1757
Deed 24 July 1760

Stewart, John   Warrant   16 May 1757
640 acres on south side Haw R., about 3 miles of
Dovers Folly; joins Wm Marsh, includes improve-
ments of Robert Marsh.
Entered 29 (Torn) 1756
Surveyed 1 Oct 1757
Deed 25 July 1760

Shaddock, Henry   Warrant   16 May 1757
640 acres on south side Deep R., includes Henry
Shaddock's improvements & where John Robeson now
lives.
Entered 29 Sept 1756
Surveyed 29 June 1757

Linchicome, Gedion   Warrant   16 May 1757
640 acres on both sides of Bakers Cr., adj "James
Bowie's south line & the place where he now
lives..." "including the place where he now
lives." On reverse side Gideon Linchicome's name
interlined & Jas Bowie written below.
Entered 2 Oct 1756
Possibly Surveyed 25 June 1757

Conner, John   Warrant   26 May 1757
640 acres on Couches Br waters of the Enoe R.
between Mathew Couches & Gilbert Strahorn.
Entered 29 Sept 1756
Deed 29 July 1760

Churton, William   Survey   7 June 1757
275 acres on both sides head branches of Dutchman's Cr. waters of Enoe, on the path to Andrew
Mitchell's and the Town of Corbinton; Jno Conner,
John Hunter: SCC.

Nelson, Thos.   Survey   8 June 1757
430 acres on Enoe & Stones Cr., begin at Edward
Stones corner oak on Gov. Johnston's line; Edward
Stone, Michal Waldrop: SCC.

Strahorn, Gilbert   Survey   9 June 1757
570 acres on Prestwoods Cr.; Joshua Stroud, Thos.
Oden: CB.
Entered 6 Oct 1755

Couch, William   Survey   9 June 1757
630 acres on the rich fork or main branch of lower
Cr., waters of Enoe; Edward Stone, Thos. Couch:
CB.

Churton, William   Survey   10 June 1757
280 acres on the head of Spirit Br waters of Eno,
adjoins Hugh Wood; Jno Conner, Hugh Wood Overseer:
SCC.
Entered 9 May 1753

Jackson, Isaac   Survey   13 June 1757
280 acres on both sides Eno R., joins Alexander
Carson; Saml Moony, Wm Jackson: SCC.
Entered 2 Oct 1754

Erwin, Robert   Survey   20 June 1757
217 acres on the south west side Enoe R. on both
sides the Old Courthouse Road; James McGowin,
Junr, George Ruminger: SCC.
Entered 9 Dec 1755

Shaddock, Henry   Survey   29 June 1757
310 acres on south side Deep R., joins Shaddock;

Wm Dawson, John Brantley: SCC.
Entered 29 Sept 1756

Burt, John   Survey   1 July 1757
  640 acres on Stirrup Iron & Briar Cr.; Edward Hopson, John Pitts: CB.

Kimbrough, Nathaniel   Survey   2 July 1757
  252 acres on Bartens Cr.; Martin Dunn, Leonard Leftear: SCC.
  Entered 9 Mar 1757

Terrel, Robert   Survey   4 July 1757
  269 acres on "uper" Bartons Cr.; Micajah Picket, James Rennals: SCC.

Stewart, John   Survey   1 Aug 1757
  640 acres on south side Haw R., joins Wm Marsh, John Marsh; Joseph Foushe, Thomas North: SCC.
  Entered 29 Sept. 1756.

Day, Mary, Jr.   Survey   11 Aug 1757
  656 acres on Cane Cr., joins Cate, Pollock; Robert Cate, Joseph Cate: CC.

Brewer, Sackfield   Survey   12 Aug 1757
  570 acres on Watery Fork of Cane Cr.; Thos Cate, Junr., John Dean: SCC.

Stroud, John, Junr.   Survey   13 Aug 1757
  522 acres on Watery Fk. of Cane Cr., on Meban's line; Thos Cate, John Edwards: SCC.

Husband, Herman   Survey   17 Aug 1757
  587 acres on waters of Sandy Cr. called the Treblile union Tract, joins Walker; Saml Walker, Thos Copestick: SCC.
  Entered 14 Nov 1754 – ("Treble Union Tract")

Field, Jane   Survey   19 Aug 1757
  286 acres on both sides of Quaker fork waters of Alamance, joins Capt. Nation; Christopher Nation, Robert Field: SCC.
  Entered 3 Nov 1755

Husband, Herman   Survey   20 Aug 1757
  (640 acres?) on waters of Sandy Creek & Rocky River called Levels addition tract joins Husband; Abraham Vanderpool, Joseph York: SCC.
  Entered 13 Mar 1755

Mackin, Alexander   Warrant   14 Sept 1757
  640 acres on Plumb Tree Cr. a fork of Buck(?) Cr. that runs on the east side of Haw R. joining Cullen Pollock's line, includes his improvements.
  Entered 26 June 1757.
  "NB ye Surname is McCrakon"
  Surveyed 21 Sept 1758.

Key, Henry   Warrant   14 Sept 1757
  640 acres on waters of New Hope called the Peach Orchard & where Mr. Gibson lived above Benjamin Bolling's line
  Entered 1 Aug 1757
  Possibly deeded 2 Apr 1761

Rainey, William   Warrant   14 Sept 1757
  640 acres on west side Haw R., joins Philips & Michl. Holt.
  Entered 10 July 1757.

Walton, Nathaniel   Warrant   14 Sept 1757
  640 acres on Middle Fk. of Little R., includes land of John Murdock.
  Entered 13 June 1757
  Surveyed 26 May 1758
  Deed 15 July 1760

Crawford, James   Warrant   14 Sept 1757
  640 acres on both sides Buffalo Cr. waters of Deep R, includes William Tomlinson's improvements.
  Entered 7 June 1757
  Deed 2 Aug 1760

Cate, John, Junr.   Warrant   14 Sept 1757
  640 acres on both sides of Cain Cr. below the Piney mountain at the lower end.
  Entered 24 June 1757
  Deed 30 July 1760

Denny, William   Warrant   14 Sept 1757
  640 acres on north side Reedy Fork, joins John Boyd, includes William Dunn's improvements.
  Entered 10 Jan 1757
  Deed 22 Feb 1759

Winborne, William   Survey   27 Sept 1757
  140 acres on Pocket Cr. & Deep R.; Richard Mauldin, Zachariah Yarborough: SCC.
  Entered 7 May 1757.

Marsh, John   Survey   30 Sept 1757
  636 acres on south side Haw R., on Little Cr.; John Stewart, Wm Marsh: SCC.

Brewer, Henry   Survey   8 Oct 1757
  585 acres on Terrels cr.; Charles Clenten, Benjamin Walker: SCC.
  Entered 9 Mar 1757

Cate, John   Survey   12 Oct 1757
    478 acres on north side of Haw R. both sides of
    Cane Cr., joins Meban & Lindley; Thos Cate Senr,
    Joseph Cate: SCC.

Jackson, William   Survey   13 Oct 1757
    480 acres on the head branches of New Hope; Owen
    Thomas, James Thomas: SCC.

Mitchell, Andrew, Esq.   Survey   14 Oct 1757
    237 acres on head branches of New Hope; John
    Hunter, John Creague: SCC.
    Entered 10 Oct 1755

Sherrod, Thomas   Warrant   5 Nov 1757
    640 acres on south side Deep R., includes Thomas
    Nobles improvements.
    Entered 5 Nov 1757
    "to Eng. for Richd Mauldin to survey"
    "to be done immediately - Lewis has got the money"
    Date "2 Mar 1761" appears on reverse - could be
    date Deed Issued

Cox, Hermon   Warrant   7 Nov 1757
    640 acres, joins his own land on Narrow Mouth Cr.
    waters of Deep R.
    Entered 7 Nov 1757
    Surveyed 8 Oct 1759
    Deed 1 Aug 1760

Freeman, Gabriel   Warrant   7 Nov 1757
    640 acres on both sides of Deep R., includes his
    improvements; on outside "Rowan & Orange."
    Entered 7 Nov 1757
    Surveyed 30 June 1758
    Deed 26 Oct 1759

Cox, Samuel   Warrant   7 Nov 1757
    640 acres on Cox's Mill Cr., waters of Deep R.,
    joins John Cox & William McPherson.
    On Reverse "Saml Cox Deep River, to be in the name
    of Joseph Comner - 7 November 1757"
    Entered 7 Nov 1757
    Deed to J. Comber - 3 Feb 1761

Alred, Soloman   Warrant   7 Nov 1757
    640 acres on Bush Creek, includes improvements of
    Alexander McDaniel.
    Entered 7 Nov 1757
    Surveyed 15 Oct 1759
    Assigned to Luke Smith

Cantrel, Joseph   Survey   9 Nov 1757
    157 acres on Toms Cr. waters of Stoney Cr.; John
    Phillips, John Cantrel: SCC.

Entered 8 June 1756

Kincheloe, John   Survey   10 Nov 1757
    252 acres on forks of Stoney Cr waters of Haw R.;
    Joseph Tanner, John Robinson: SCC.

Norton Stephen   Warrant   10 Nov 1757
    640 acres on both sides Mayo Cr., joins Donald-
    son's upper line.
    Entered 4 Nov 1757
    Deed 2 Jan 1761.

Bynam, John   Warrant   10 Nov 1757
    640 acres on New Hope Cr., begin on Benjamin
    Clements line. "N.B. This is the second Warrt. out
    for the above land, the former being loss, or in
    the Surveyors Hand. Let it be surveyed directly.
    Fra. Corbin - and both Warrants returned with the
    Plans."
    Entered 6 Nov 1755
    Assigned to John Falconer
    Surveyed 6 Mar 1761

Morgan, Mark, Capt.   Survey   14 Nov 1758
    640 acres on New Hope; James Beesley, Bendel
    Straughan: SCC.

Sterret, James   Survey   17 Nov 1757
    250 acres on Roses Cr. waters of north fork of Haw
    R., joins Tillot or Simmons; Robert Gwain, Wm
    Kennedy: SCC.
    Entered 28 Feb 1757

Hargrove, Richard   Survey   19 Nov 1757
    520 acres on south side North Fork of Haw R.,
    joins Peter Dillon; Alexandr Nelson, George Nel-
    son: SCC.

Brown, David   Survey   24 Nov 1757
    475 acres on waters of Great Alamance, Qualls Br.,
    joins Clapp, Davis or Cussick on county line; John
    McGowin, John McDonnel: SCC.

Rainey, William   Survey   1 Dec 1757
    591 acres on west side Haw R., joins Michal Holt,
    Phillips; John Rennols, David Phillips: CC. 2
    copies.

McKee, Anne   Survey   5 Dec 1757
    378 acres in fork of Little R., adjoins James
    Mordack, John Dunagan, Allison, Wm Boggan; James
    Mordack, James McCarver: CB

Conner, John   Survey   20 Dec 1757
    365 acres on branches of Stones Cr., adjoins Chur-

ton; Gilbert Strahorn, Lazarus Benton: SCC.
Entered 29 Sept 1756

Reed, William, Esq.   Survey   28 Dec 1757
488 acres on Nunns Mill Cr., joins Wm Combs, Reed, Thomas Wiley, Nunn, crosses Bigg Cr.; John Slater, Wm Combs: SCC.

Holt, Michal   Survey   29 Dec 1757
739 acres on waters of Little Alamance, on McCullock's line, Phillips Spring Br.; Jacob Holt. Frederick Brock: SCC.

Holles, Moses   Survey   14 Jan 1758
162 acres on north side of Dann R., joins Gowing, Mayor; Enoch Robinson, Alexr. Gowing: SCC.
Entered 26 Apr 1757

Blakely, James   Warrant   26 Jan 175
640 acres on both sides Flatt R., on upper end of Osborn Jeffreys lower survey.
Entered 6 Sept 1757
Surveyed 14 May 1760
Deed 2 Feb 1761

Paine, James, Col.   Warrant   26 Jan 1758
640 acres, joins his own plantation on Deep Cr., includes improvements of John Taber & Great Spring.
"Execution of the above warrant having been prevented by the late disturbances I do hereby Validate it for six months longer - Edenton 20 Feb 1760."
Surveyed 2 Aug 1760
"Warrant rec. from Sherwood Haywood 5 Feb 59."
Deed 30 Jan 1761

Talbert, James   Survey   27 Jan 1758
552 acres on waters of Rich Land Cr., joins Lawrence Vanhuck; John Hues, Garrit Neal: SCC.
Entered 27 Sept 1756.

Sergant, William   Survey   31 Jan 1758
200 acres on both sides of Sergant Cr.; Stephen Sergant, Benjamin Hide: SCC.

Long, Benja   Survey   1 Feb 1758
490 acres on both sides Storeys Cr., joins Thos. Laxton; James Long, John Newton: SCC.

Dixson, Henry   Survey   2 Feb 1758
640 acres on both sides Adams Cr.; Benja Long, James Long: SCC.

Dickson, Micheal   Survey   2 Feb 1758
640 acres on both sides Adam's Cr.; Benj. Long, James Long: CB.

Norton, Stephen   Survey   6 Feb 1758
410 acres on both sides Little Cr. a branch of Mayo, joins Donelson; Zach Smith, John Powell: SCC
Entered 4 Nov 1757

Poe, Stephen   Warrant   17 Mar 1758
640 acres on waters on New-Hope Cr., joins Francis Day, begin on the Bank of Rocks.
Entered 2 Nov 1757
Assigned to Richard Straughan
Surveyed 11 Oct 1758

King, John   Warrant   17 Mar 1758
640 acres on waters of new Hope begin on his own line called the Timber Tree Slack.
Entered 31 Oct 1757
Surveyed 6 May 1758

Bird, James   Warrant   17 Mar 1758
640 acres on the headwaters of Enoe, joins on the north and west side of Wilkin's land.
Entered 1 Nov 1757
"Removed to Staggs Cr. ye waters of Buck Cr.
Surveyed 22 Sept 1758
Deed 24 July 1760

Jones, Francis   Warrant   17 Mar 1758
640 acres on a branch of Haw R., on south side, below Cain Cr., about a mile of William White's, Daniel Cole's claim.
Entered 2 Nov 1757.
"Francis Jones to Joseph McLester - Removed to the middle ground between Ferrels Cr. and Dry Cr. west side Haw R."
Deed 2 Aug 1760

Hunter, John   Warrant   20 Mar 1758
500 acres, begin about a mile above mouth of Buffalo
Entered 9 June 1752
Deed 14 May 1757 "in Blake Baker's name"
"Jno Hunter then Bashire now Blake Baker"

King, John   Survey   6 May 1758
524 acres on waters of New Hope, joins Capt. Lloyd; Henry Morris, Thos. Oden: SCC.
Entered 31 Oct 1757

Morgan, Mark, Capt.   Survey   8 May 1758
682 acres, joins Mulkey & Morgan; John Barby, James Rigsby: SCC.
Entered 4 Nov 1756

Walton, Nathaniel   Survey   26 May 1758
    402 acres on Middle Fk. of Little R., joins
    Rutherford; Archalus Wilson, Robert Berry: SCC.
    Entered 15 June 1757.

Fuller, Joseph   Survey   5 June 1758
    322 acres in the fork of Deep R. & Rocky R.; Lewis
    Brantley, Moses Ginn: SCC.

Piles, John   Survey   7 June 1758
    243 acres on south branches of Cain Cr. & both
    sides ye road from Cane Cr. to Cape Fair; Francis
    Jones, Hugh Laughlin: SCC.

Husband, Herman   Survey   30 June 1758
    402 acres on Deep R. called Cedar Falls; Abram.
    Buckles, Filman Culp: CC.
    Entered 14 Nov 1754

Brashear, Robert Samuel   Survey   9 July 1758
    381 acres on North & South Buffelo, adjoins John
    McNight, Donnels; Robt. Brashear Senr., Jesse
    Brashear: CB.

Carragan, John   Survey   22 July 1758
    304 acres on south side of Enoe R. on Spirit Br.
    Joins Willy, Jackson, Hugh Wood; Jonathon Grinels,
    Robert Mororaty: SCC.

Holdman, Richard   Warrant   (Torn) Aug 1758
    640 acres on south side Flatt R., joins Hercules
    Wilson & Philemon Bradford.
    Entered (Torn) 1758
    Surveyed 15 May 1760
    Deed 2 Feb (Torn)

Taber, John   Warrant   (Torn) Aug 1758
    640 acres, Begin on (torn) Pryor's line, both
    sides Mayo's Cr.
    Entered (Torn) 1758
    Surveyed 2 Aug 1760
    Deed (Torn) Feb 176(Torn).

Hembre, David   Warrant   1 Aug 1758
    640 acres on both sides Blue Wing Cr. Begin at
    mouth of a Great Br. below Hembree's plantation.
    Entered 14 Apr 1758
    Surveyed 22 July 1760
    Deed 31 Jan 1761

Shaw, Benjamin   Warrant   1 Aug 1758
    640 acres on south side of Flatt R., begin on
    Robert Cate's line, include Griffin Humphrey's
    improvements.
    Entered 26 Jan 1758

    Surveyed 28 July 1760
    Assigned to Saml. Ffarmer
    Deed 9 Feb 1761

Tapley, Hosea   Warrant   1 Aug 1758
    640 acres on both sides of Mountain Br., includes
    Adam Tapley's improvements.
    Entered 18 Jan 1758
    Surveyed for John Camp 9 Aug 1760
    Deed 2 Feb 1761

Alridge, Joseph   Warrant   1 August 1758
    640 acres on both sides Flatt river, joins John
    Cate's line. "The execution of the above warrant
    having been prevented by the late disturbances, I
    do hereby validate it for six months longer..."
    Edenton 20 Feb 1760
    Entered 14 Mar 1758
    Surveyed 29 July 1760
    Deed Jan 1761

Black, Peter   Warrant   1 Aug 1758
    640 acres on both sides of a branch of Mayo,
    includes George Him's(?) improvements.
    Entered 17 Feb 1758
    Surveyed 20 May 1760

Goforth, Miles   Warrant   1 Aug 1758
    640 acres on both sides South Hico, adjoins his
    own land.
    Entered 14 Mar 1758
    Deed 30 Jan 1761

Barnett, Joseph   Warrant   1 Aug 1758
    640 acres on both sides Gant Cr.
    Entered 30 Dec 1757
    Deed 31 Jan 1761

Cox, Soloman   Warrant   5 Aug 1758
    640 acres on Little Brush Cr. above his own Place.
    Entered 5 Aug 1758 - Assigned to Peter Youngblood
    1 Apr 1760.
    Surveyed 12 Sept 1760
    Deed 2 Feb 1761.

Cox, Samuel   Warrant   5 Aug 1758
    640 acres on Richland Cr. at mouth of Batchelor's
    Cr.
    Entered 5 Aug 1758
    Surveyed 10 Oct 1759
    Deed 1 Aug 1760

McCrackon, Alexander   Survey   21 Sept 1758
    318 acres, joins Pollock's line ye north side ye
    old Courthouse Road, Both sides Plum Creek; David

Bradford, James Bird: SCC.

Bird, James   Survey   22 Sept 1758
   388 acres on Staggs Cr. waters of back Creek;
   Alexander McCrackon, David Bradford: SCC.

Combs, William   Survey   28 Sept 1758
   181 acres on Mountain Cr. waters of Flatt R.,
   joins Churton; James Horton, Joseph Parker: SCC.
   Originally surveyed for John McCormick. McCormick's name is erased and Wm Combs' name inserted.

Torintin, Alexander   Survey   29 Sept 1758
   369 acres on waters of Little R.; James Cheek, Wm
   Young: CC.
   Deed Feb 61.

Stewart, John   Survey   3 Oct 1758
   640 acres on south side Haw R. on Robinson Cr.;
   Willm Petty, Phillip Hodgens: SCC.

Strahghan (Straughan), Richard   Survey   11 Oct 1758
   357 acres on Prestwoods Cr. waters of New Hope,
   joins Francis Day; John Barby, Henry Key: SCC.

Churton, William   Survey   2 Nov 1758
   460 acres on south side Enoe R., on Dutchman Cr.,
   on both sides Patterson Path, adj. Col. Corbin;
   Edwd. Stones, Wm Combs: CB.

Craford, Jas (James)   Warrant   3 Nov 1758
   640 acres on Ridge between N Hico & the County
   Line, on the head of Dobbins Br. Includes his own
   improvements.
   "July ye 31st 1759 Recd 0:4:0 in full"
   Entered 27 May 1752

Morgan, Mark, Capt.   Survey   4 Nov 1758
   640 acres on New Hope, joins his line; James
   Beesley, Bendal Straughan: SCC.

Morgan, Mark, Capt.   Survey   14 Nov 1758
   640 acres on New Hope; James Beesley, Bendel
   Straughan: SCC.

Morgan, Mark, Capt.   Survey   15 Nov 1758
   640 acres on New Hope & Morgans Cr., joins his own
   line; James Beesley, Bendal Straughan: SCC.
   Entered 4 Nov 1756

Coxs, Willm   Warrant   10 Dec 1758
   640 acres on Deep R. above Benj. Williams improvements & below Crafford.
   Entered 11 Sept 1753

Jones, Charles   Warrant   6 Feb 1759
   640 acres on the head of Seven Mile Br., adjoining
   on the south side of Thos. Whitehead.
   Entered 3 Sept 1758
   "To Day Son Christn Nam Blank"
   Deed 30 Jan 1761

Teague, Edward   Warraant   6 Feb 1759
   640 acres on branches of Rocky R. near Timothy
   Terrel, former possession by Joshua Beasley.
   Entered 14 Sept 1758
   Surveyed 26 May 1759
   Deed 18 July 1760.

Reed, William, Esq.   Warrant   6 Feb 1759
   640 acres on both sides Deep R., joins Searcy's
   upper line, includes Thomas Graves improvements &
   mouth of Flatt Cr.
   Entered 1 Aug 1758
   "This Warrant Changed by Mistake by one that is
   Deeded already."

Teague, William   Warrant   6 Feb 1759
   640 acres joins Willm Vernon Land being the place
   he lives on near Timothy Terrel.
   Entered 18 Nov 1758
   Surveyed 26 May 1759
   Deed 18 July 1760

Kerksey, Christopher   Warrant   6 Feb 1759
   640 acres on Wilkinsons Cr. on north side Haw R.
   Entered 17 July 1758
   Surveyed 25 Oct 1759
   Deed 30 July 1760.

Brooks, Joel   Warrant   6 Feb 1759
   640 acres on west side of Haw, joins John Jones &
   John Wright, includes his improvements.
   Entered 13 Sept 1758
   Surveyed 23 May 1759(?)
   Deed 2 Aug 1760

Cantrel, Isaac   Warrant   6 Feb 1759
   640 acres on north east side of Haw below Collins
   Creek adjoining Henry Warson and Robert Cates.
   Entered 18 July 1758
   Surveyed 27 Oct 1759(?)
   Deed 30 July 1760

Barbee, Joseph   Warrant   6 Feb 1759
   640 acres on Sicamore Fork of Crabtree where the
   creek is about two yards over.
   Entered 11 Sept 1758
   Surveyed 20 Sept 1759

Wiley, William   Warrant   6 Feb 1759
   640 acres on north fork of North Allamance, both
   sides Miry Br., runs toward Clapps line.
   Entered 12 Sept 1758
   Surveyed 30 Nov 1759
   Deed 3 Feb 1762

Dunagan, John   Warrant   6 Feb 1759
   640 acres on Little R., adjoins Capt. Synnot.
   Entered 9 Aug 1758
   Deed 2 Feb 1761

Poe, Stephen   Warrant   6 Feb 1759
   640 acres on west side Haw R., adjoins Argalus
   Henderson.
   Entered 12 Sept 1758
   Surveyed 23 oct 1759

Mafitt, William   Warrant   10 May 1759
   640 acres on br. of Rich Cr., joins Thomas Cox, on
   Tibbs Runn, waters of Rich Cr.
   Entered 10 May 1759

Brown, Daniel   Warrant   10 May 1759
   640 acres on south west side of Deep R., joins
   William Cox.
   Entered 10 May 1759
   Surveyed 13 Oct 1759(?)

Graves, William   Warrant   10 May 1759
   640 acres on the forks of Little Brush Cr., about
   a mile below Solomon Cox.
   Entered 10 May 1759
   Deed 3 Feb 1761

Brooks, Joel   Survey   23 May 1759
   488 acres on west side of Haw both sides of Cane
   Cr., joins William Nelson, Stanfield; Wm Wright,
   Joseph Wright: CC.

McLester, Joseph   Survey   24 May 1759
   127 acres on west side Haw R., on middle ground
   between Ferrels Cr. & Dry Cr.; Wm Basket, James
   Ashmore: CB.
   Entered 2 Nov 1757
   On reverse - "Francis Jones to Joseph McLester -
   127 acres"
   2 copies of survey

Teague, William   Survey   26 May 1759
   160 acres on New Graden Road to Cape Fair, joins
   William Varnell; Solomon Terrel, Wm Varnel: CC.

Teague, Edward   Survey   26 May 1759
   405 acres on New Garden Road near Terrels; Wm
   Varnel, Soloman Terrel: CC.

Crawford, James   Survey   1 June 1759
   201 acres on south side Deep R. on Buffelo or
   Tomlins Cr.; John Campbell, Matthew Campbell: CC.
   Entered 17 June 1757

Torrington, Samuel   Warrant   11 July 1759
   640 acres on mouth of Buffalo, joins Margt. Bog-
   gan, omits spring adjoining Boggan.
   Entered 11 May 1759
   Surveyed 27 Oct 1760
   "a Dispute with Nathl Cary & not to goe over Thos.
   Wade old line"
   Deed 27 Jan 1761

Lapslie, Thomas   Warrant   11 July 1759
   640 acres on east side of Zachary Kaddle's land on
   waters of Back Cr.
   Entered 22 June 1759

Terrell, Robert   Warrant   11 July 1759
   640 acres on both sides of great Lick Creek, joins
   McCulloh's supposed line.
   Entered 10 June 1759
   Surveyed 29 Nov 1760
   Assigned to John Alston
   Deed 9 Feb 1761

Martin, Zachariah   Warrant   11 July 1759
   640 acres on both sides Rocky R. on the Capefear
   Rd., where he now lives.
   Entered 12 June 1759
   Surveyed 20 Oct 1759
   Deed 31 Jan 1761

Cox, Wm   Survey   31 Aug 1759
   350 acres on New Hope, near Pattersons Path; Edward Stone, Thos. Couch: CB.

Barbee, Joseph   Survey   20 Sept 1759
   393 acres on both sides Sycamore Creek of Crabbtree; Wm Roberts, Ratlif Foyel: SCC.

Kimbrough, Nathaniel   Survey   21 Sept 1759
   516 acres on Sicomore Cr waters of Crabbtree;
   Joseph Barby, Wm Holifield: CC. "N.B: by a warrant
   Joseph Barby.

Cox, Harmon   Survey   8 Oct 1759
   224 acres on north side Deep R., joins his own
   line; Eleazer Hunt, John Cox: CC.

Scarlett, John   Survey   8 Oct 1759
   349 acres on a br. of Cox Mill Cr. waters of Deep

R., joins Wm McFerson, Wm Cox; Harmon Cox, Benja. Cox: CC.

Husband, Herman   Survey   9 Oct 1759
245 acres, called Harmonia Union, on Deep R., joins Peter Youngblood; Harmon Cox, Eleazer Hunt: CC.

Wierman, Nicholas   Survey   10 Oct 1759
221 acres on Richland Cr., joins Benjamn. Cox; Saml. Cox, Thos. Cox: CC.
Entered 14 June 1755.

Cox, Samuel   Survey   10 Oct 1759
430 acres on Richland & Batchelor's Cr.; Thos Cox, Benjamn Cox: CC.

Mafitt, William   Survey   11 Oct 1759
130 acres on Tibbs Run waters of Richland Cr.; Thos Cox, John Cox: CC.

Brown, Daniel   Survey   13 Oct 1759
595 acres on south side of Deep R., joins William Cox; Thos Cox, Arthur Mundy: CC.

Alred, Soloman   Survey   16 Oct 1759
400 acres on both sides of the mouth of Sandy Creek, Begin on Deep River on Hopkin's line; George Julian, John Alred: CC.

Martin, Zachariah, Jr.   Survey   20 Oct 1759
339 acres on both sides Rocky R. & Cape fair Road; Woolrick White, John White: CB.

Poe, Stephen   Survey   23 Oct 1759
194 acres on west side Haw R.; John White, Simon Poe, Jr.: CC. 2 copies.

Kerksey, Christopher   Survey   25 Oct 1759
429 acres on north side of Haw R. on Wilkinsons Cr.; Nathan Melton, Jas Kerksey: CC.
Entered 17 July 1758

Melton, Nathan   Survey   25 Oct 1759
391 acres on north side Haw R.; Robert Patterson, John Collins: CC.
Entered 4 Nov 1756

Cantrell, Isaac   Survey   27 Oct 1759
115 acres on north east side of Haw R. below Collins Cr., joins Henry Warson, Robt. Cates; Reson Nelson, James Cantrel: CC.
Entered 18 July 1758

Sharp, Joseph   Survey   10 Nov 1759
478 acres on both sides Enoe R., joins James Armstrong, Robert Erwin, Joseph Maddock, Thomas Stubbs, James Taylor; Nathaniel Walton, Jacob Walter: CC.

Mitchell, David   Survey   13 Nov 1759
144 acres on Negroe Cr., joins Hugh Dobbins; John McManamy, John Barnett: CC.
Entered 15 (?) 1756.

Mateer (Mateere), Robt.   Entry   13 Dec 1759
640 acres on Simmons Cr., joins John Cunningham. Signed "William Mateer for Robert Mateer."

Mateer, Robert   Warrant   13 Dec 1759
640 acres on Simmons Cr., joins John Cunningham.

Mateer, William   Warrant   13 Dec 1759
700 acres on waters of Haw R., betwixt two creeks called Troublesome, on east side of river, crossing mouth of Little Troublesome Cr.
Deed 4 Feb 1761

Phillips, Benjamin   Entry   13 Dec 1759
700 acres on upper forks of Little Alamans, joins Michel Holt, Sr.

Philips, William   Entry   13 Dec 1759
(David Philips) interlined
700 acres on south side Haw R., above old trading ford.

Phillips, William   Warrant   13 Dec 1759
700 acres on south side Haw R., about a mile above the old trading ford.
Deed 2 Oct 1761

Frazier, John   Survey   14 Dec 1759
300 acres, joins Joseph Maddock, Churton, Taylor; Robert Reed, Thomas Stubbs: CC.
Entered 5 Mar 1758

Morris, George   Entry   22 Dec 1759
700 acres on Lower Bartons Cr., includes John Clark's Mill.

Hobson, Georgge, Jr.   Warrant   1 Jan 1760
640 acres on forks of Rocky R., joins George Hobson, Sr.
Deed 2 Feb 1761

Swift, Thomas   Warrant   3 Jan 1760
600 acres on waters of Sandy Cr., joins Herman Husband, includes plantation where Swift now lives.
Surveyed 20 July 1760

Deed 2 Oct 1761

Barbe, Joseph Entry 5 Jan 1760
700 acres on a br. of New Hope called the Northeast, adjoins his own & Capt. Morgan's lines.

Boid, John Warrant 7 Jan 1760
700 acres on Deep R. begin about a quarter mile above Duncan Bohannon on south side of river.
Surveyed 23 June 1761(?)
Deed 2 Oct 1761

Smith, Edward Warrant 10 Jan 1760
700 acres on Aldange's Cr., a br. of Flatt R., includes Thos. Edward's plantation.
Surveyed 23 June 1760
Deed 6 Feb 1761

Holyfield, William Entry 1 Feb 1760
640 acres on upper Bartons Cr. about 2 miles above Nathaniel Kimbrough's land. Signed William "O" Holyfield.

Holyfield, William Warrant 1 Feb 1760
640 acres on upper Barton Cr. about two miles above Nathaniel Kimbroughm.
Surveyed 5 Feb 1760 (On reverse "Surveyed 5 Feb 1761")

Aldridge, Nathaniel Entry 1 Feb 1760
500 acres on the Bushey Fork of Flatt River begin where Thomas Robisons line crosses So Fork on the North side, signed "Nathaniel + Aldrige."

Aldridge, Nathaniel Warrant 1 Feb 1760
500 acres on Bushey Fork of Flatt River.
Surveyed 29 July 1760
Deed 6 Feb 1761

Holyfield, William Survey 5 Feb 1760
700 acres on upper Barton Cr.; John Smith, Samuel Jenkins: CC. 2 copies

Thomas, John Warrant 3 Feb 1760
700 acres on Deep Cr. waters of Flat R., joins Danl. Weldon.
Surveyed 8 Aug 1760

Fulton, Samuel Entry 13 Feb 1760
700 acres on Deep Cr. waters of Flatt R., begin at a pine about a quarter mile above where he now lives.

Fulton, Samuel Warrant 13 Feb 1760
700 acres on Deep Cr. waters of Flatt R., includes his plantation.
Surveyed 21 June 1760
Deed 9 Feb 1761

Thomas, John Entry 13 Feb 1760
700 acres on Deep Cr., waters of Flatt R., adjoins Daniel Weldon, signed with a mark.

Cate, John Entry 14 Feb 1760
600 acres on Flatt R. begin at James Dickens cor. joining Robert Cates line and the river includes Griffen Humphrays improvements, signed John + Cate.

Cate, John Warrant 14 Feb 1760
600 acres on Flat R. begin at James Dickings's cor., includes Griffin Umphries improvements. "This land was taken away by Benj. Shaw."

Bullock, Richard Warrant 15 Feb 1760
640 acres on Elleby's Cr waters of Neuse, begin on Mr. McCullock line.
Surveyed 27 Nov 1760
Deed Feb 1761

Bullock, Richard Entry 15 Feb 1760
640 acres on Elebys Cr. joins upper line of his former entry made this day.

Alston, John Entry 15 Feb 1760
700 acres on both sides Little Lick Cr., waters of Neuse. Begin on Mr. McCulloch's line.

Alston, John Entry 15 Feb 1760
700 acres on Great Lick Cr., waters of Neuse, adjoins Mr. McCulloh.

Stone, Edward Entry 16 Feb 1760
600 acres on waters of Eno, joins Thomas Nelson, signed with a mark.

Vernal, William Entry 18 Feb 1760
700 acres on branches of Little R. & Flatt R., adjoins John White, includes improvements by one Parker.

Vernal, William Warrant 18 Feb 1760
700 acres on the branches of Little R. & Flat R., adjoins John White, includes a small improvement possessed by one Parker.
Surveyed 26 July 1760
Deed 2 Feb 1761

Bledsoe, Jacob Warrant 18 Feb 1760
700 acres on upper Bartons Cr. the waters of

(Torn), includes his own improvements.
Surveyed 26 Feb 1760

Few, William   Warrant   20 Feb 1760
640 acres on both sides the Enoe R., joins William Gorss's line.
Entered 26 Oct 1759
Deed 22 Jan 1761

Burgamy, William   Warrant   20 Feb 1760
640 acres on Lower Barton Cr., begin whereon Clark lives.
Entered 19 Sept 1759
Surveyed for Nathaniel Kimbrough 4 Feb 1761
Assigned to Sherrod Rennals 9 Feb 1761

Dunnagan, John   Warrant   20 Feb 1760
640 acres on Deep Cr. a fork of Flatt R. including Thomas Collins, George Gibson, Paul Collins Mulatto Improvements.
Entered 30 Sept 1759
Surveyed 20 June 1760
Deed 3 Feb 1761

Lemmon, Henry   Warrant   20 Feb 1760
640 acres on or near head of Dutchman above Wrightman Place.
Entered 23 Sept 1759
Surveyed - No Date

Bledsoe, Jacob   Survey   26 Feb 1760
680 acres on Upper Barton Cr.; Wm Holifield, Richd Massey: CC. 2 copies

Laxson, Thomas   Survey   28 Feb 1760
381 acres on Country Line Cr., joins Joseph Dolittle; James McDanold, John Lay: SCC.

Wharton, William   Warrant   8 Mar 1760
640 acres on Deep Cr. waters of Flatt R., joins Thomas Gibson, includes plantation where Thomas Collings now lives.
Surveyed 21 June 1760
Deed 2 Feb 1761

Womack, Jacob   Warrant   11 Mar 1760
700 acres on Mayho Cr., begin on Mayho's upper corner running to Robt. McFarlin's line, include vacant land betwen McFarlin & Hugh Barnet.
Surveyed 23 July 1760
Deed 6 Feb 1762

Brantley, Joseph   Warrant   11 Mar 1760
700 acres on south side Deep R., begin about 1/4 mile below plantation whereon John Brantley lives, includes sd. plantation.
Surveyed 25 Feb 1761
Deed 2 Oct 1761

Taylor, Edward More   Entry   11 Mar 1760
700 acres on north fk. of Flatt R. between William Jay & Hosea Tapley, includes his own improvements.

Saxon, Benjamin   Entry   11 Mar 1760
700 acres on the North East Branch of New Hope, joins John Martin.

Saxon, Benjamin   Warrant   11 Mar 1760
700 acres on the north east branch of New Hope, joins John Martin.
Surveyed 10 July 1760

Taylor, Edward More   Warrant   11 Mar 1760
700 acres on north fork of Flatt R. between William Jay & Hosea Tapley, includes his own improvements.
Surveyed 23 June 1760
Deed 6 Feb 1761

Humphrays, William   Entry   11 Mar 1760
700 acres on Neuse R., includes his own improvements, signed "Wm Humphys."

Humphries, William   Warrant   11 Mar 1760
700 acres on Neuse R., includes his own improvemeants.
Surveyed 31 Jan 1761

Kirk, Joseph   Warrant   18 Mar 1760
700 acres on south side Haw R. in the forks of Haw R. & Deep R., includes plantation Kirk lives on.
Surveyed 1 Sept 1760
Deed 2 Oct 1761

Nelson, Abraham   Entry   25 Mar 1760
600 acres on waters of Enoe on Stone Cr., joins Edward Stone, signed: Abraham "A" Nelson.

Nelson, Abraham   Warrant   25 Mar 1760
600 acres on waters of Enoe on Stone Cr., joins Edward Stone.
Deed 5 Feb 1761

Jeffreys, Osborn by John Allen Sharp Entry 5 Apr 1760
700 acres on Flatt R., joins surveys of Jeffreys.

Jeffreys, Osborn   Warrant   5 Apr 1760
700 acres on waters of Flatt R. joins several surveys of land now possessed by sd. Jeffreys lying on the forks of Flat R. on both sides the

Middle or North Fork.
Surveyed 30 Oct 1760
Deed 7 Feb 1761

Yarbrough, Samuel   Warrant   10 Apr 1760
640 acres on Mayho Cr., joins Phillip Pryor.
Surveyed 24 July 1760
Deed 2 Feb 1761

Rickets, Reason   Entry   21 Apr 1760
400 acres on waters of new Hope, begin about a quarter mile above the mouth of Long Br., both sides of Bakers Cr., signed with a mark.

Person, Thomas by William Churton, Esq.
                         Entry   21 Apr 1760
700 acres on Dials Cr. of Flatt R., near William Horton.

Rickets, Reason   Warrant   21 Apr 1760
400 acres on waters of new Hope, begin about a quarter mile above the mouth of Long Br., both sides Bakers Cr.
Surveyed 16 Feb 1761
Deed 2 Oct 1761

Goforth, Miles   Survey   5 May 1760
472 acres on South Hico, adjoins William Wilson; Ezekiel Dolarhide, Aquilla Dollarhide: CB.

Blakely, James   Survey   14 May 1760
362 acres on flatt river, adjoins Osborn Jeffryies; Samuel Fulton, Benj. Morrow: CB.

Holeman, Richard   Survey   15 May 1760
(Torn) acres, Joins said Holeman, Robt. Cates, Archillus Willson; Archillus Wilson, Joseph King: SCC.

McGowin, John   Warrant   16 May 1760
640 acres on both sides Piney Mountain Cr. waters of New Hope, on west side of Jas. Bowie place.
Entered 29 Sept 1756
"at Wileys"
"for Waldrope"
Deed 5 Feb 1761

Black, Peter   Survey   20 May 1760
102 acres on Maho Creek; Peter Black, Peter Craven: SCC.

Warrin, Henry   Survey   2 June 1760
642 acres on both sides Bartons Cr., joins William Barnes; Wm Roberts, Wm Barnes: CB.

Taber, John   Entry   9 June 1760
700 acres on Philip Pryor's line, both sides Mayho Cr.

Tabor, John   Warrant   9 June 1760
700 acres, adjoins Philip Pryor, on Mayho Cr.
"Voided by a former entry the money returned - Jas Watson."

Brooks, Thomas   Entry   10 June 1760
640 acres on Rocky R., at lower end of island foard.

Roberts, Richard   Entry   10 June 1760
700 acres on south fk. of Cubb Cr. waters of Tarr R begin near head of cr.

Roberts, Richard   Warrant   10 June 1760
700 acres on south fk. of Cubb Cr. waters of Tarr R., begin near head of cr.
Surveyed 4 Feb 1761

Baker, Andrew   Warrant   19 June 1760
640 acres on a drain of Kemps Br., waters of Neuse, adjoins Osborne Jeffreys.
"To Timothy Shaw - Living on the Land"
Surveyed 31 Jan 1761

Baker, Andrew   Entry   19 June 1760
640 acres on drains of Kemp Br., waters of Neuse, adjoins Osborn Jeffreys.

Dunagin, John   Survey   20 June 1760
330 acres on both sides Deep Cr.; Wm Vernal, Thos Dunagin: SCC.

Wharton, William   Survey   21 June 1760
190 acres on both sides Deep Cr.; joins Dunagin, Thos. Gibson; Thos. Collins, George Gibson: SCC.

Fulton, Samuel   Survey   21 June 1760
520 acres on both sides Deep Cr., joins John Dunagin; James Blakely, William Wharton: SCC.

Smith, Edward   Survey   23 June 1760
390 acres on a br. of Flatt R.; John Sattorfield, Edwd Smith: SCC.

More, Edward   Survey   23 June 1760
(Taylor, Edward More)
375 acres on both sides Flatt R., joins Hosea Tapley, Wm Jay; John Satterfield, Ed Smith: SCC.

Higdon, John, Jr.   Entry   24 June 1760
700 acres on Reedy Cr., 3/4 miles above mouth,

crosses Crabtree Cr., signed with a mark.

Bracewell, Richard by William Bracewell
Entry   28 June 1760
640 acres on Deep R., adj. Thomas Tucker, includes falls near Hodges For(torn), signed with mark.

Humphreys, Wm.   Survey   31 June 1760
516 acres on west side Neuse R., on Crooked Cr., joins Christopher Marr; Jacob Bledsoe, Ann. Colson: CC. Date first written as 31 Jan 1760

Carson, John   Survey   3 July 1760
337 acres on the head branches of Bigg Cr. waters of Enoe, joins William Combs; Joseph Maddock, Thomas Graves: CC. 2 copies

Saxon, Benjamin   Survey   10 July 1760
660 acres on the North East Fk. of new Hope, joins George Martin; Geo. Herndon, Wm Roberts: CC. 2 copies

Bollin, Alexander   Survey   17 July 1760
458 acres on both sides Rattlesnake Cr.; David Terry, Alexr Bollin: CB.

Swift, Thomas   Survey   20 July 1760
260 acres on waters of Sandy Cr. called Swifts Choices, joins Herman Husband; Thos Welborn, Enos Stimson: CC.

Hart, David   Survey   20 July 1760
292 acres on a fork of the South Fork of the Country Line Cr.; Nathl Hart, Thos Hughs: SCC.

Hembre, David   Survey   22 July 1760
690 acres on Blewwing Cr.; Seth Pettypool, Robt Sanfield: SCC.

Womack, Jacob   Survey   23 July 1760
282 acres on Mayho Cr.; joins Mayho & Hugh Barnet & Robt. Macfarland; Jacob Womack, Robt. Macfarland: SCC.

King, Peter   Entry   23 July 1760
640 acres on Dials Cr. waters of Flatt R., begin near the cabon where he now lives, signed Peter "P" King.

King, Peter   Warrant   23 July 1760
640 acres on Dials Cr. waters of Flatt R. begin near the cabbin where he now lives.
Surveyed 7 Dec 1760 for 543 acres

Yarbrough, Samuel   Survey   24 July 1760
476 acres on both sides Maho Cr.; joins Phillip Pryor; John Webb, Ed Isom: SCC.

Carrinton, John   Warrant   24 July 1760
700 acres on Flatt R. begin on Thos. Gibsons line
Surveyed 6 Dec 1760

Carinton, John   Entry   24 July 1760
700 acres on Flatt R., adj. Thomas Gibson, signed by mark.

Bird, Burgon   Survey   24 July 1760
455 acres on a branch of the Meadows of Tarr R. No CC. listed.

Dickens, James   Entry   25 July 1760
700 acres on Flatt R., adjoins James Bowie, signed with a mark.

Dickens, James   Warrant   25 July 1760
700 acres on both sides Flatt R., adjoins James Bowie.
Surveyed 5 Dec 1760
On reverse - "Whereas Richd Parsons has made me full satisfaction for the within warrant I do hereby give up the property fully to him & Desire it may be returned in his name witness my hand - 5th Day of Dec 1760 - Jas. Dickens (his mark) - Witness: John Lea"
Returned in Richd Parsons name for 360 acres.

Vernal, Wm   Survey   26 July 1760
399 acres on a branch of Little R.; James Blakely, Charles Gibson: CB.

Farmer, Samuel   Survey   28 July 1760
581 acres on both sides Flatt R., joins James Dickins, Robt. Cates, Richd Holeman; Archillus Willson, Richd Holeman: SCC.

Aldridge, Nathaniel   Survey   29 July 1760
220 acres on Bushey Fork of Flatt River, adj. Thomas Robinson; Joseph Aldrige, John Hague: SCC.

Alridge, Joseph   Survey   29 July 1760
295 acres on both sides of Flatt R., Joins John Cate; Nathaniel Aldrige, John Reedman: SCC.

Haley, David   Warrant   30 July 1760
700 acres on Cane Cr the north side of Dan R., begin on Mayo's line at his off sett, along the Country line.
Surveyed 16 Dec 1760
Assigned to John Rainey 16 Dec 1760, wit: John Lea.

Barnet, Joseph   Survey   31 July 1760
    210 acres on both sides Gants Cr.; Hambleton Ronnels, James McNight: CB.

Churton, William   Survey   2 Aug 1760
    550 acres on south side Enoe R. on the back side of Occanecha Mountains & on the west side Francis Corbins Esq land; Rob Reed, John Gray: SCC.

Rennals, Sherrod   Survey   5 Aug 1760
    337 acres on Lower Barton Cr.; Benjn. Ward, Aaron Johnson: CC.

Dunagan, John   Survey   6 Aug 1760
    392 acres on both sides of Little R., joins Michael Synnot, Joseph Ellison, & Robt. Wilson; Thos Dunagan, Thos Resane: SCC.

Thomas, John   Survey   8 Aug 1760
    519 acres on both sides Deep Cr., joins Daniel Weldon; James Blakeley, Benj. Morrow: SCC.

Nelson, Abraham   Survey   8 Aug 1760
    450 acres on both sides of a fk. of Edward Stone's Cr., joins Edwd Stone; Thomas Nelson, Andrew Kenady: SCC.

Camp, John   Survey   9 Aug 1760
    210 acres on both sides of Mountain Cr waters of Flatt R.; Isom Milton, John Camp: SCC.

Sherrod, Thomas   Survey   9 Aug 1760
    400 acres on south side Deep R. on Pretty Cr., joins Armstrong; Richd Mauldin, Benja Mauldin: CC. 2 copies.

Bledsoe, John   Survey   12 Aug 1760
    400 acres on both sides Neuse R., joins Wm Humphrey and a line called McCullock's (Note: Land lay in both Johnston and Orange Counties); Moses Bledsoe, Aaron Bledsoe: CC. 2 copies

Bohannon, Duncan   Survey   12 Aug 1760
    450 acres on south side of Deep R., adj. Nathl. Powell, Lord Granville's line, Smith's Cr.; Jos. Fuller, John Britt: CB. (2 copies)

Waldrop, Michael   Survey   12 Aug 1760
    370 acres on waters of New Hope; Thomas Nelson, John Nincho: SCC.

Key, Henry   Survey   13 Aug 1760
    450 acres on Bones Cr. (Benja. Bowlings Cr.), joins Benja. Bowling; Wm Picket, Henry Willis: CC.

Churton, William   Survey   15 Aug 1760
    290 acres on both sides of Seven Miles Br. and Trading Path. Begin at a Hicory saplin on Cullen Pollock's line; Willm Reed Esq., Will Reed Junr.: SCC.

Copeland, James   Warrant   19 Aug 1760
    700 acres on south side Haw R., begin at mouth of Stinking Cr.
    Surveyed 2 Feb 1761
    Deed 2 Oct 1761

Sarjent, William   Entry   19 Aug 1760
    700 acres on Milston Cr. waters of Hico, joins Joseph Sutton, signed: William "X" Sarjent.

Kirby, William   Entry   19 Aug 1760
    700 acres on little bush Creek, waters of New Hope, between Falconer & Clemons, both sides of cr., signed "William Kerby"

Sarjeant, William   Warrant   19 Aug 1760
    700 acres on Milston Cr. waters of Hico, joins Joseph Sutton.
    Surveyed 21 Jan 1761.

Whitton, George by Ann Smith   Entry   19 Aug 176(Torn)
    700 acres on the Little Cr., waters of Deep R., signed with a mark.

Embree, John   Warrant   19 Aug 1760
    700 acres on south fork of Little R., begins on Capt. Synnot's line.
    Surveyed 2 Dec 1760

Booker, John   Warrant   19 Aug 1760
    600 acres on Buck Horn, adj. Robert Jones.
    Surveyed 5 Mar 1761.

Booker, John   Entry   19 Aug 1760
    600 acres on Buckhorn Cr., adj. Robert Jones, signed with mark.

Kimbrough, Nathl.   Survey   19 Aug 1760
    400 acres on horsenapp br., waters of Crabtree, adj. Kimbrough; Wm Cardon, Martin Dunn: CB. 2 copies

Copeland, James   Entry   19 Aug 1760
    700 acres on south side Haw R., mouth of Stinking Cr.

Walliace, Josias   Entry   20 Aug 1760
    700 acres on Fork Cr., waters of Deep R., includes plantation where Enoch Spinks now lives, signed

with a mark.

Marten, William by Zachariah Marten   Entry   20 Aug 1760
   700 acres on Dry Cr., waters of Haw R., where he
   now lives.

Davie, Gabriel   Warrant   22 Aug 1760
   700 acres on Mayho Cr. begin on John Gordons line,
   joins his own line.
   Surveyed 23 Oct 1760
   Deed 27 Jan(?) 1761

Lemmone, Henry   Survey   22 Aug 1760
   246 acres on Head Branches of Dutchman Cr. alias
   Cantrile Cr.; John Hunter, Henry Hasting: SCC.

Parker, Richard, Esq.   Warrant   22 Aug 1760
   700 acres on Pokeberry Cr. waters of New Hope.
   Surveyed 8 Feb 1761
   Deed 2 Oct 1761

Lapsley, Thomas   Survey   22 Aug 1760
   250 acres on drains of Back Cr., joins Jacob
   Riley, Edward Linche; James Bird, Jacob Riley: CC.

Parker, Richard, Esq.   Entry   22 Aug 1760
   700 acres on Pokeberry Cr. of Haw R.

Saxon, Benjamin   Survey   27 Aug 1760
   640 acres on the North East Fk. of New Hope, joins
   Saxon, Saml. Saxon; Geo. Herndon, Wm Roberts: CC. 2
   copies.

Herndon, George   Survey   30 Aug 1760
   500 acres on North East fork of Newhope waters,
   adjoins Benj. Saxon; Benj. Saxon, Wm Roberts: CC. 2
   copies.

Mecteere, William   Survey   (No Day)Sept 1760
   337 acres on both sides Beaver Dam Fork of Haw R.,
   joins John Boyd; Willm Potter, James Harrot: SCC.

Saxon, Charles   Entry   1 Sept 1760
   700 acres on Beaverdam Swp. waters of rocky R.,
   joins John Landrum, includes plantation where
   Saxon lives.

Saxon, Charles   Warrant   1 Sept 1760
   700 acres on Beaverdam Swp. waters of Rocky R.,
   joins John Landrum, includes plantation where
   Saxon now lives.
   Surveyed 1 Mar 1761
   Deed 2 Oct 1761.

Cox, William   Entry   Tueth Day Sept 1760
   700 acres on Enoe R., joins his own & William
   Few's line, signed with a mark.

Poplin, George   Entry   2 Sept 1760
   700 acres on Bear Cr., waters of Rocky R., where
   he now lives, signed with a mark.
   Surveyed (?) - 24 June 1761
   Deed 2 Oct 1761

Poplin, George   Warrant   2 Sept 1760
   700 acres on Bear Creek, waters of Rocky R., where
   he now lives.

Kirk, Joseph   Survey   5 Sept 1760
   375 acres on south side Haw R., joins Copeland's
   Island, Kirk's Cr.; Jno Brantley, Geo. Kirk: CC.

Lawrence, John   Survey   6 Sept 1760
   412 acres on Great Alamance waters of Haw R.,
   begin about a mile above Brother Peter's line;
   Nich Bunrick, Peter Sharemore: SCC.

Spinks, Enoch   Warrant   8 Sept 1760
   700 acres on Fork Cr. of Deep R., begin near
   Corbel's lake, include his mill & plantation.
   Surveyed 8 Mar 1761
   Deed 2 Oct 1761

Spinks, Enoch   Entry   8 Sept 1760
   700 acres on Fork Cr. of Deep R., begin near
   Corbel's lake, includes his mill & plantation.

Gardner, John   Warrant   8 Sept 1760
   700 acres on Richland Cr waters of Deep R., about
   a half mile above the mouth of the cr., includes
   his improvements.
   Surveyed 1 Feb 1761
   Deed 2 Oct 1761

Hobson, George, Jr. Survey   9 Sept 1760
   620 acres in fork of Rocky R., adjoins George
   Hobson, Sr.; David Vestal, Stephen Hobson: CB.

Brantley, Joseph   Survey   10 Sept 1760
   650 acres on south side Deep R., adjoins Duncan
   Bohannon, John Brantley; Joseph Kirks, George
   Wooten: CC.

Fikes, Malachy   Warrant   10 Sept 1760
   700 acres on Phils Cr. waters of New Hope, joins
   Reed and Maden, includes plantation where John
   Hinchy now lives.
   Surveyed 1 June 1760
   Deed 2 Oct 1761

Comber, Joseph   Survey   10 Sept 1760
    370 acres on Cox's Mill Cr. on west side of Deep
    R., joins Wm Cox & McParson; Solo. Cox, Peter Cox:
    SCC.

Fikes, Malachy, by Joseph White   Entry   10 Sept 1760
    700 acres on Phils Cr. waters of New Hope, joins
    William Reed, John Maden, includes plantation
    where John Hinchie now lives.

Youngblood, Peter, Jr. Survey   10 Sept 1760
    349 acres both sides Little Bush Cr.; Solom. Cox,
    John Fanning: SCC.

Mecteere, Robert   Survey   11 Sept 1760
    231 acres on both sides Roses Cr. of the Beaver
    Dam Fork of Haw R., joins Giles Tillet; James
    Harratt, James Mecteere: SCC.

Graves, William   Survey   12 Sept 1760
    401 acres on Little Brush Cr.; Peter Youngblood,
    James Fanning: SCC.

McGowen, Peter   Entry   30 Sept 1768
    700 acres on Elebys Cr., near Poplar Spring Br.,
    signed with a mark.

Patterson, Robert   Entry   1 Oct 1760
    700 acres on waters of Haw R. betwixt Red Field
    Cr., includes 2 plantations his own improvements,
    Signed: Robert "R P" Patterson.

Patterson, Robert   Warrant   1 Oct 1760
    700 acres on waters of Haw R. betwixt Redfield Cr.
    & Mile Cr., on Mile Cr., joins Edward Kirksey,
    includes 2 plantations his own improvements.
    Surveyed 6 Apr 1761
    Deed 2 Oct 1761

Denny, James   Entry   6 Oct 1760
    700 acres on waters of Enoe on Seven Mile Cr. &
    Moors Br. begin on William Goss's line, signed
    James X Denny.

Denny, James   Warrant   6 Oct 1760
    700 acres on waters of Enoe on Seven Mile Cr. &
    Moors Br. begin on William Goss's line.
    Surveyed 23 Jan 1761
    Deed 2 Oct 1761

Purdum, John   Warrant   9 Oct 1760
    700 acres on waters of Sicamore fork waters of
    Crabtree, includes land called Rich Land.
    Surveyed 7 Feb 1761

Purdum, John   Entry   9 Oct 1760
    700 acres on waters of Sicamore fork waters of
    Crabtree, includes land called the Rich Land.

Usery, John   Entry   18 Oct 1760
    700 acres on Gents Cr. waters of Hico, joins
    Burges Harrel & Michel Dickson, includes improve-
    ments of William Chambers.

Usery, John   Warrant   18 Oct 1760
    700 acres on Gents Cr. waters of Hico, joins
    Burges Harrel & Michel Dickson, includes improve-
    ments of William Chambers.
    Surveyed 24 Apr 1761
    Deed 14 Oct 1761

Ellidge, Isaac   Warrant   20 Oct 1760
    700 acres on a br. of Rocky R., adjoins Ambros
    Smith, where Elledge lives.
    Surveyed 6 Apr 1761
    Deed 6 Dec 1761

Elledge, Isaac, by Shedrik Jacobs   Entry   20 Oct 1760
    700 acres on a br. of Rocky R., begin on Ambros
    Smith, plantation where he now lives, signed Shad-
    rack Jacob.

Edwards, John   Entry   20 Oct 1760
    700 acres on Marks Cr., waters of New Hope joins
    Thomas Durham & John Price, where he now lives,
    signed with mark.

Jacobs, Shedrick(Shadrack) by Isaac Ellidge
                        Entry   20 Oct 1760
    700 acres on a br. of Rocky R., adjoins Ambros
    Smith, where Jacobs now lives.

Edwards, John   Warrant   20 Oct 1760
    700 acres on Marks Cr. waters of New Hope, joins
    Thomas Durham & John Price, includes plantation he
    now lives on.
    Surveyed 5 Apr 1761
    Deed 2 Oct 1761

Hartso, Philip   Entry   22 Oct 1760
    500 acres in Fork betwixt Rocky R. & Nix Cr.,
    includes plantation he now lives on.

Davy, Gabriel   Survey   23 Oct 1760
    519 acres on waters of Maho, joins John Gordon &
    Davy; Thos Striplen, Geo Flinn: SCC.

Martin, Zachariah, Jr. Entry   24 Oct 1760
    700 acres on Dry Cr., waters of Haw R., includes
    Wood's & Lune's improvements.

Claton, Benone by Powel Benbo   Entry   24 Oct 1760
    500 acres on Meadow Cr., waters of Rocky R.,
    includes Samuel Culverson's improvements, Benbo
    signed with a mark.

Claton, Benone   Warrant   24 Oct 1760
    500 acres on Meadow Creek, waters of Rocky R.,
    includes Samuel Culverson's improvements.
    Surveyed 23 April 1761
    Deed 2 Oct 176(Torn)

Torrington, Samuel   Survey   27 Oct 1760
    394 acres in the fork of Little R. & Buffalo Cr.,
    joins Margaret Boggan, James Cheek, John Brown;
    Richd Holeman, Alexr Torrington: SCC.

Cantrell, Isaac   Survey   27 Oct 1759
    115 acres on north east side of Haw R. below
    Collins Cr., joins Henry Warson, Robt. Cates;
    Reson Nelson, James Cantrel: CC.
    Entered 18 July 1758

Jeffries, Osborn   Survey   30 Oct 1760
    480 acres on both sides flatt R., joins his sever-
    al former tracts, Jas. Blakley, Joseph Mumford;
    Wm Pittman, Saml. Pittman: CB.

Few, William   Survey   3 Nov 1760
    280 acres on the west side Enoe R., joins his own,
    Mr. Watson's & Wm Cox's line; James Scarlet, John
    Wood: SCC.

Carter, Finch   Survey   5 Nov 1760
    210 acres on a fork of the Double Cr., waters of
    So. Hico, adj. Samuel Sirrat.; Hambleton Ronols,
    Allen Sirrat: CB.

Day, Francis   Survey   13 Nov 1760
    418 acres on the head of Seven Mile Cr. and Pea
    Cr., adjoins Whitehead, Capt. Synnot, Fincher;
    Gideon Linchicum, Amos Whitehead: CC. On Back
    "Francis Day by warrant of Charles Jones."

Dennis, John   Warrant   18 Nov 1760
    700 acres on the heads of Buckquarter, begin at
    his own cor., includes Dutch George & Peters im-
    provements (on Enoe R.).
    Surveyed 26 May 1761
    Deed 2 Oct 1761

Copland, Nicholas by James Copland   Entry   18 Nov 1760
    700 acres on waters of Haw. R. begin near the head
    of Little Creek, includes the plantation he now
    lives on, signed "Jeames Copland for Nicholas
    Copland."

Hinton, William   Warrant   18 Nov 1760
    700 acres on the fork of Lick Cr joining Earl
    Granville's line & John Rickels.

Dennis, John   Entry   18 Nov 1760
    700 acres on Heads of Buck Quarter, Begin on his
    own corner & includes Dutch George & Peters im-
    provements.

Copland, Nicholas   Warrant   18 Nov 1760
    700 acres on waters of Haw R., begins near head of
    Little Cr.
    Surveyed 10 May 1761
    Deed 2 Oct 1761
    On reverse at bottom "June 13th 1761" ?

Bridges, James   Entry   18 Nov 1760
    700 acres on Mudd Br., waters of Flatt R., signed
    with a mark.

Hinton, William by Nathaniel Cary   Entry   18 Nov 1760
    700 acres in fork of Lick Cr., joins Earl Gran-
    ville's line & John Rickets.

Sellars, James   Entry   19 Nov 1760
    700 acres on Pinetree Cr., waters of Haw R.,
    adjoins Nathan Melton, where Sellars now lives.

Talbot, Joseph by John Lea   Entry   19 Nov 1760
    700 acres on Forks of Storys Cr., waters of Hico.

Sellers, James   Warrant   19 Nov 1760
    700 acres on Pine Tree Cr., waters of Haw R.,
    joins Nathan Melton, where he now lives.
    Deed 2 Oct 1761

Talbert, Joseph   Warrant   19 Nov 1760
    700 acres on the forks of Morys Cr., waters of
    Hico.
    Surveyed 27 Dec 1760

Brooks, Joab   Entry   19 Nov 1760
    700 acres on waters of Rocky R. on branches of
    Tick Cr. & Meadow Cr., includes his improvements.

Craven, Petert   Entry   25 Nov 1760
    700 acres on Deep Cr., waters of Flatt R., adjoins
    John Bumpas's line.

Craven, Peter   Warrant   25 Nov 1760
    700 acres on Deep Cr., waters of Flatt R., joins
    John Bumpass.
    Surveyed 27 Jan 1761
    Deed 14 Oct 1761

Bullock, Richard   Survey   27 Nov 1760
   570 acres on Ellebees Cr. waters of Nuce, begin on
   McCullochs line, joins Robert Abercromby; Zachariah Bullock, Wm Bullock: CC.

Alston, John   Survey   29 Nov 1760
   500 acres on Great Lick Cr., adjoins McCulloch's
   line; Arnold Russel, Wm Reeves Junr.: CB.

Embree, John   Survey   2 Dec 1760
   256 acres on south fork of Little R., joins Michl
   Synnot, Josh Allison, John Dunagin; Enos Elliman,
   John Elliman: SCC.

Holyfield, Ralph   Entry   3 Dec 1760
   700 acres on Sicamore Cr., waters of Crabtree,
   includes his own improvements, signed with a mark.

Terrel, Timothy by Jacob Bledsoe Entry 3 Dec 1760
   700 acres on 3rd fork of New Hope, near path from
   Pattersons to Alstons.

Bledsoe, Jacob   Entry   3 Dec 1760
   700 acres on White Oak Cr., waters of Haw R.

Holyfield, Ralph   Warrant   3 Dec 1760
   700 acres on Sicamore Cr., waters of Crabtree.
   Surveyed 7 Feb 1761

McWhorter, George   Entry   4 Dec 1760
   600 acres on Deep Cr. waters of Flat R., begin
   below John Bumpas, includes improvements called
   Arnold's Folly.

Barnet, Thomas   Entry   4 Dec 1760
   200 acres on Laxton's Cr., waters of Hico, joins
   west side of Laxton's Survey. Signed with a mark.

McWhorter, George   Warrant   4 Dec 1760
   600 acres on Deep Cr. waters of Flat R., begin
   below John Bumpass, includes improvements called
   Arnold's Folly.
   Surveyed 3 Feb 1761 for 450 acres.

Barnet, Thomas   Warrant   4 Dec 1760
   200 acres on Laxton's Cr. the waters of Hico, on
   west side of Laxton's Survey, includes a small
   improvement.
   Surveyed 25 Apr 1761
   Deed 14 Oct 1761

Parsons, Richd.   Survey   5 Dec 1760
   360 acres on Flat River adjoins (Torn) Bowie;
   Shadrick Dickens, Richd Parson: CB.

Carrington, John   Survey   6 Dec 1760
   581 acres on Flat R.; Absolem Baker, Robt Graves:
   SCC.

King, Peter   Survey   7 Dec 1760
   543 acres on Dials Cr waters of Flatt R., joins
   James Horton, Mr. McCullough's line; Absalom Baker, John Carrington: SCC.

Landrum, John by Richard Copeland Entry 13 Deec 1760
(John Landrum, Jr.)
   700 acres on Mill Cr., waters of Rocky R., adjoins
   John Landrum, Sr.

Landrum, John   Warrant   13 Dec 1760
   700 acres on Mill Cr., waters of Rocky R., adjoins
   John Landrum, Sr.
   Surveyed 12 June 1761
   Deed 2 Oct 1761

Landrum, Benjamin   Warrant   13 Dec 1760
   700 acres on Mill Cr. waters of Rocky R. begin
   near the head of the creek, includes his own
   improvements.
   Surveyed possibly 2 July 1761
   Deed 2 Oct 1761

Landrum, Benjamin   Entry   13 Dec 1760
   700 acres on Mill Cr. waters of Rocky R., signed
   by Jas. Watson.

Rainey, John   Survey   16 Dec 1760
   290 acres on north side Dan R. & on Cain Cr. begin
   at a pine on the Country or province line, joins
   Mayo; David Haley, David Terry: SCC.

Brown, John   Warrant   26 Dec 1760
   700 acres on Flatt River, includes Bolins, Ridles
   & Colins improvements.
   Surveyed 13 April 1761
   Deed 14 Oct 1761

Talbert, Joseph   Survey   27 Dec 1760
   655 acres on both forks of Stories Cr.; James
   Talbert, Abram Miles: CB.

Haley, David   Warrant   27 Dec 1760
   700 acres on Ridge between Rattlesnake Cr. &
   Country line Cr., begin at a pine marked DH,
   includes Runnal's Cabins.
   Surveyed 29 July 1761
   Deed 14 Oct 1761

Colins, Thomas   Warrant   29 Dec 1760
   700 acres on Dials Cr. waters of Flatt R.

Surveyed 13 Apr 1761
Deed 13 Oct 1761

Ramsey, John   Warrant   30 Dec 1760
700 acres on Mill Cr., waters of Rocky R., near John Landrum, Jr., includes Peter Salingers improvements.
Surveyed 3 June 1761
Deed 2 Oct 1761

Shaw, Timothy   Survey   1 Jan 1761
700 acres on drains of Kemo Br. & the head of Crooked Cr., adjoins Osborn Jeffries, Humphries; Vincent Jones, Prid(?) Willis: CC.

Husband, Herman   Entry   11 Jan 1761
700 acres on a br. of Sandy Cr., waters of Deep R., adjoins his own line, includes improvements of Ebenezer Starns, William Walker & John Fields.

Booth, Daniel   Warrant   16 Jan 1761
700 acres on Barbies Cr., waters of New Hope, betwixt Rachel Barbie's & John Booth's lines.
Surveyed 1 July 1761

Sargent, William   Survey   21 Jan 1761
210 acres on the Mill Cr. of South Hico, joins Darbey Hunley; Joseph Gold, Steven Sargent: SCC.

Denny, James   Survey   23 Jan 1761
375 acres on Pea Cr., waters of Enoe, adjoins Goss, Moors Br., Denny; Gideon Linchicum, John Scarlet: CB.

Long, John   Warrant   27 Jan 1761
700 acres on Castle Cr., waters of Hico, joins John Hurley, includes his own & his father's improvements.
Surveyed 25 July 1761
Deed 6 Dec 1761

Tapley, Hosea   Warrant   29 Jan 1761
700 acres on Muddy Br. waters of Flatt R., joins his former survey.
Surveyed 9 Apr 1761
Deed 14 Oct 1761

Bauldry, William   Entry   2 Feb 1761
300 acres on south side Tar R., begins at John Hardee's corner, near the pole bridge br., signed Willm Bauldry. No county given on entry.

Copeland, James   Survey   2 Feb 1761
275 acres above Stinking Cr., on Haw R.; Jno. White, Wm Copeland: CB.

McWhorter, George   Survey   3 Feb 1761
450 acres on Deep Cr.; Thomas Striplin, James Collins: SCC.

Roberts, Richard   Survey   4 Feb 1761
700 acres on Cubb Cr.; Wm Wharton, Willis Roberts: SCC.

Gardner, John, Capt.   Survey   5 Feb 1761
500 acres on Deep R. & Richland Cr.; Jno Lawrence, Jno Needham: CC.

Purdum, John   Survey   7 Feb 1761
500 acres on branches of the east fork of Sycomore waters of Crabbtree; Samuel Jinkins, Richd Massey: CC. 2 copies.

Holyfield, Ralph   Survey   7 Feb 1761
300 acres on Sycamore Cr., waters of Crabtree; Wm Holyfield, Richd. Massey: CB.

Parker, Richard, Esq.   Survey   8 Feb 1761
345 acres on Pokeberry Cr., joins his land; James Sellers, Wm Griffin: CC.

Lea, John   Warrant   9 Feb 1761
700 acres on Richland Cr waters of Hico, joins his own line includes Brooks improvements.
Surveyed 7 Sept 1761
Assigned to Wm Brooks
Deed 6 Dec 1761

Freeman, William   Entry   10 Feb 1761
700 acres. No Description, signed with a mark.

Talbert, James   Warrant   16 Feb 1761
700 acres on Richland Cr. waters of Hico, joins James Anderson, includes improvements where John Talbert now lives.
Surveyed 14 Aug 1761
Deed 14 Oct 1761.

Rickets, Reason   Survey   16 Feb 1761
450 acres on Bakers Cr. waters of New Hope, joins John Patterson, Bohannon, Wm Rhoads; Edward Stone, John Castlebury: CC.

Shepherd, Andrew   Warrant   17 Feb 1761
700 acres on Big Lick Cr. on northwest side of Cap Fair R., includes Arthur Taylor's improvements.
Surveyed 18 June 1761
Deed 2 Oct 1761

Satterfield, Bedwel   Warrant   17 Feb 1761
700 acres on Richland Spring Cr., joins James

Satterfield, includes his own improvements.
Surveyed 8 Apr 1761
Deed 13 Oct 1761

Bledsoe, John   Warrant   17 Feb 1761
700 acres on White Oak Cr., waters of New hope, on both sides Cape Fair Rd.
Surveyed 12 Aug 1761

Davis, Adam   Warrant   17 Feb 1761
700 acres on Haw R. including the vacant land betwixt William Philips and the McCullochs line.
Assigned to John Campbell
Deed 2 Sept 1761

Bridges, James   Warrant   17 Feb 1761
700 acres on north fork of Cubb Cr. waters of Tarr R.
Surveyed 14 April 1761
Deed 13 Oct 1761

Hogg, Gideon   Warrant   18 Feb 1761
700 acres on Greens Cr waters of Dann begin on the Country Line, includes his own improvements.
Surveyed 13 Aug 1761
Deed 6 Dec 1761

Harvey, William   Warrant   19 Feb 1761
700 acres on a branch of Richland Cr, waters of Deep R., includes his own improvements.
Surveyed 17 July 1761
Deed 2 Oct 1761

Hinton, William   Survey   23 Feb 1761
600 acres on a fork of Lick Cr. on the south west side of Cape fair, adjoins Lord Granville's line, Enoch Lewis; Richd Brazel, Wm Brazel: CC. 2 copies

Saxon, Charles   Survey   1 Mar 1761
400 acres on Beaver Dam Cr. waters of Rocky R., joins Landrum; Richd. Copeland, Richd. Burk: CC.

Scarlett, John   Warrant   2 Mar 1761
700 acres on Enoe R., betwixt Thomas Nelson & James Couch, on both sides of river.
Surveyed 28 May 1761
Deed 2 Oct 1761

Fikes, Malachy   Survey   5 Mar 1761
438 acres on Phils Cr waters of New Hope, joins Michael Waldrop, Reed; John Hinche, Michael Waldrop: CC.

Booker, John   Survey   5 Mar 1761
375 acres on Buckhorn Cr., adj. Robert Jones & Jacob Leavin; Jacob Leavin, Wm Brown: CB.

Bumpass, Samuel   Warrant   5 Mar 1761
700 acres on Spring Br., waters of Flatt R., both sides Spring Br. & Mudd Br.
Surveyed 11 Apr 1761
Deed 13 Oct 1761

Thomason, William Turnor Warrant   5 Mar 1761
700 acres on White Oak Cr., waters of New Hope.
Surveyed 5 Sept 1761

Reeves, William, Jr.   Warrant   5 Mar 1761
700 acres on Stirrupiron Cr., waters of Crabtree, includes Francis Decern's improvements.
Surveyed 4 Sept 1761

Barker, Thomas   Warrant   6 Mar 1761
700 acres on White Oak Swp., begin on William Utlys line.
Surveyed 2 Sept 1761
Deed 6 Dec 1761

Rawls, Dempsey   Warrant   7 Mar 1761
700 acres on White Oak Cr., waters of New Hope, below William Turnor Thomason.
Surveyed 2 Sept 1761
"Elisha Cane to direct this Survey"

Spinks, Enoch   Survey   8 Mar 1761
225 acres on fork Cr., waters of Deep R.; James Lawrence, James Letham: CB.

Lewis, Enoch   Warrant   9 Mar 1761
700 acres on Buckhorn Cr., waters of Capefair, joins Henry Shaddock.
Surveyed 2 Sept 1761

Nunn, William   Warrant   9 Mar 1761
700 acres on both sides New Hope Cr., joins Mark Morgan & Luke Bynum.

Bumpass, John   Warrant   10 Mar 1761
700 acres on Deep Cr., waters of flat R., begins at the Road where it crosses the creek.
Surveyed 9 Apr 1761
Deed 6 June 1761

Davie, Gabriel   Warrant   10 Mar 1761
700 acres on Byas Mill Cr. waters of Mayho, includes his own improvements.
Surveyed 16 Apr 1761
Deed 13 Oct 1761

Moffitt, Hugh   Warrant   11 Mar 1761

700 acres on fork of Little Brush cr., waters of Deep R.
Deed 2 Oct 1761

Bracewell, Henry   Warrant   16 Mar 1761
700 acres on south side of Cape Fear R. begin at Hector McNeil's lower corner
Surveyed 15 Sept 1761

McGee, John, Capt.   Warrant   19 Mar 1761
700 acres on a br. of Sandy Run waters of Deep R., includes Jacob Flay's & Widow Ham's improvements.
Deed 2 Oct 1761

McGee, John, Esq.   Survey   19 Mar 1761
180 acres on a br. of Sandy Cr. waters of Deep R., joins Herman Husband; Thos. Welborn, Jacob Jones: CC.

Poplin, George   Survey   23 Mar 1761
550 acres on Bear Cr., waters of Rocky R.; George Williams, Jno Miles: CB.

Mullen, John   Warrant   24 Mar 1761
700 acres on Lick Fork of Hogan Cr., begin at John Thrasher's line, includes his own & Thomas Mullen' improvements.
Surveyed 21 Sept 1761
Deed 6 Dec 1761

King, John   Warrant   26 Mar 1761
700 acres on Roberson's Cr waters of Haw R., begin on Charles Foushee's cor., includes the plantation where the widow Foushee now lives.
Surveyed 17 June 1761

Smith, George   Warrant   26 Mar 1761
700 acres on north side Haw R., where he lives.
Surveyed 24 Sept 1761
Deed 6 Dec 1761

Poe, Stephen   Warrant   31 Mar 1761
700 acres on south side Haw R., joins his former survey, includes his own & his father's improvements.
Surveyed 16 June 1761
Deed 2 Oct 1761

Walker, Samuel   Warrant   31 Mar 1761
700 acres on South Hico, joins Thomas Langley & William Wilson, includes improvements he now lives on.
Surveyed 10 Sept 1761
"Signed over to Edwd Camp"
Deed 6 Dec 1761

Patterson, Gilbert   Warrant   2 Apr 1761
700 acres on south side Deep R., joins Zachariah Martin's upper corner, includes his own improvements.
Surveyed 25 Sept 1761
Deed 6 Dec 1761

Welborn, William, Junr.   Warrant   3 Apr 1761
700 acres on Mcintires Cr., waters of Deep R.
Surveyed 18 July 1761
Deed 2 Oct 1761

Edward, John   Survey   5 Apr 1761
265 acres on Marks cr., joins Thomas Durham, John Price; James Hogwood, Robert Pendergrass: CC.

Yancey, James   Warrant   6 Apr 1761
700 acres on the Crooked Fk. of Aarons Cr. waters of Dann, joins John Baynes, follow the line formerly laid off for said Baynes but not returned.
Surveyed 15 Oct 1761
Deed 6 Dec 1761

Patterson, Robert   Survey   6 Apr 1761
700 acres on Mile Cr. waters of Haw R., joins Edward Kirksey; Robert Sellers, James Patterson: CC.

Satterfield, Bedwell   Survey   8 Apr 1761
92 acres on Richland Spring Cr. waters of Flatt R., joins Hosea Tapley's former line; John Arnold Jas. Satterfield: SCC.

Tapley, Hosea   Survey   9 Apr 1761
695 acres on Muddy Br. of Flatt R., joins Tapley; John Camp, Hosea Tapley Junr.: SCC.

Lowe, Thomas   Warrant   11 Apr 1761
700 acres on Tarr R., joins Robert Bumpass. "No Land To Be Found" - "Entry Money Returned."

Bumpass, Samuel   Survey   11 Apr 1761
440 acres on spring br. waters of Flatt R.; Timothy Carter, Ed Bumpass: SCC.

Brown, John   Survey   13 Apr 1761
698 acres on Flatt R., joins Thos Gilson (Gibson?); Moses Riddle, Charles Gibson: SCC.

Moor, David   Warrant   13 Apr 1761
700 acres on Forrest Cr. waters of Little R., joins James Anglen & Isaac Gaddis.
Surveyed 12 Oct 1761
Deed 6 Dec 1761

Collins, Thomas   Survey   13 Apr 1761
    700 acres on Dial's Cr. of Flatt R.; George Gibson, Paul Collins: SCC.

Craven, Thomas   Warrant   13 Apr 1761
    700 acres on Deep Cr. waters of Flatt R., begin on Peter Craven's line.
    Syrveyed 10 Oct 1761
    Deed 6 Dec 1761

Bridges, James   Survey   14 Apr 1761
    340 acres on Cubb Cr. of Tarr R., joins Absolom Lankson; Thos Striplin, John Bridges: SCC.

Davey, Gabriel   Survey   16 Apr 1761
    364 acres on north fork of Maho Cr.; John Hall, John Scott: SCC.

Lantrop, Thomas   Warrant   20 Apr 1761
    700 acres on both sides of Rocky R. includes the plantation he now lives on.
    Surveyed 26 June 1761
    Deed 2 Oct 1761

Witty, Robert   Warrant   20 Apr 1761
    700 acres on Seven Mile Cr. waters of Enoe R., includes his own improvements.
    Surveyed 13 Sept 1761

Crow, James   Warrant   20 Apr 1761
    700 acres on a prong of Phils Cr. waters of New Hope, includes his own improvements.
    Syrveyed 13 Sept 1761

Copeland, Thomas   Warrant   20 Apr 1761
    700 acres on Richland Cr. waters of Rocky R., includes the plantation he now lives on.
    Surveyed 26 Junne 1761
    Deed 2 Oct 1761

Booth, John   Warrant   20 Apr 1761
    700 acres on the northeast waters of New Hope, joins George Herinnlon's line.
    Surveyed 13 Oct 1761
    Deed(?) 3 Nov 1761

Claton, Benone   Survey   23 Apr 1761
    200 acres on Meadow Cr. waters of Rocky R.; Saml Culberson, Andw Culberson: CC.

Brashears, Midleton   Warrant   23 Apr 1761
    700 acres on south side Reedy Fork of Haw R., including William Williams improvements.
    Syrveyed 24 Sept 1761
    Deed 6 Dec (Torn)

Usury, John   Survey   24 Apr 1761
    313 acres on Gents Cr. waters of Hico, joins Michael Dickson, Humphrey Barnett, Henry Dickson, Paul Harrilson; Ed Alman, Ed Chambers: SCC

Barnett, Thomas   Survey   25 Apr 1761
    200 acres on Stories Creek, joins Thos Laxson; Henry McCoy, John Barnett: SCC.

Jenkins, David   Warrant   25 Apr 1761
    700 acres on Mill Cr. waters of Deep R., includes Robert Hodges & Christopher Hussey's Improvements
    Surveyed 18 Oct 1761
    Deed possibly issued 2 Dec 1761

Hartso, Philip   Survey   29 Apr 1761
    350 acres on Rocky R., on Nicks Cr.; Jno Swaim, Wm Swaim: CC.

Brashear, Robert   Warrant   8 May 1761
    700 acres on the Reedy Fork & Buffalo, waters of Haw R., adjoins Blake Baker's land where Bazel Brashear now lives.
    Surveyed 25 Oct 1761
    Deed 6 Dec 1761

Sellers, James   Survey   9 May 1761
    700 acres on Pine Tree Cr., waters of Haw R., adjoins Nathan Melton; Robt. Sellers, James Cater: CB.

Brooks, Joab   Survey   18 May 1761
    375 acres on branches of Tick Cr. & Meadow Cr. on the Cape Fear Rd.; Mark Brooks, Isaac Brooks: CC.

Flinn, Thomas   Warrant   19 May 1761
    700 acres on the head of Deep Cr. waters of Flatt R., begin on Doctor James Paine's line, runs toward the head of Richland Spring Cr., includes his own improvements.
    Surveyed 17 Nov 1761
    Deed 6 Dec 1761

Webb, James   Warrant   19 May 1761
    700 acres on waters of Tarr R., joins Francis Devinport & Robert Bumpas.
    "No land to be found - Being taken by an older warrant of Thos. Lowe"
    "The money Returned"

Youngblood, Peter, Jr.   Warrant   19 May 1761
    700 acres on head of Meadow Cr. waters of Rocky R. between Zachariah Martin & William Wiley formerly William Skeals.
    Surveyed 12 Nov 1761

Deed (Possibly) 4 Jan 1762

Trice, Edward   Warrant   19 May 1761
700 acres near mouth of 3rd fk. of New Hope, joins Joseph Barbie.
Surveyed 31 Oct 1761

Capper, Thomas   Warrant   20 May 1761
700 acres on mouth of Second Cr., waters of New Hope.
Surveyed 1 Oct 1761
Deed 6 Dec (Torn)

Bledsoe, Jacob   Warrant   20 May 1761
700 acres on both sides of Laurel Cr waters of Lick Cr., includes Robert Belvin's Improvements

Day, John   Warrant   20 May 1761
700 acres on Tarr R. on Samuel Yarbrough's line, includes his own improvements.
Surveyed 20 July 1761
Deed 6 Sept 1761

Jones, Nathaniel   Warrant   20 May 1761
700 acres on Watts Br., waters of Crabtree, joins Mr. Young & Francis Jones & Mr. Herring.
Surveyed 15 Oct 1761
Deed 6 Dec 1761

Hightower Austin   Warrant   20 May 1761
700 acres on both sides Morgans Cr., waters of New Hope, begins near Mr. Caswell's line, includes his own improvements.
Surveyed 18 Nov 1761

Williams, Charles   Warrant   22 May 1761
700 acres on Flatt R., begin at Osborn Jeffry's line.
Surveyed 19 Oct 1761
Deed 6 Dec 1761

Dennis, John   Survey   26 May 1761
375 acres on both sides Buckquarter and the trading path, joins Isaac Jackson; Isaac Jackson, W. Jackson: CC.

Scarlett, John   Survey   28 May 1761
700 acres on both sides Enoe R., adjoins James Couch; James Couch, Barney Cabe: CB.

Ramsey, John   Survey   3 June 1761
400 acres on a br. of Mill Cr. waters of Rocky R.; Benjn. Landrum, Wm Ramsey: CC.

Harrison, Thomas   Warrant   10 June 1761
700 acres on forks of Little Creek waters of Dann betwixt his own and Mayho's lines.
Surveyed 6 Dec 1761
Deed 6 Mar 1762

Landrum, Benjamin   Survey   12 June 1761
540 acres on head of Mill Cr. waters of Rocky R.; Timothy Terrel, Sampson Sellers: CC.

Landrum, John   Survey   12 June 1761
700 acres on south fork of Mill Cr., waters of Rocky R., Sampson Sellars, Wm Ramsey: CB.

Poe, Stephen   Survey   16 June 1761
347 acres on south side Haw R., adjoins his own line, John Stuart; Argulus Henderson, Simon Poe Junr.: CB.

King, John   Survey   17 June 1761
640 acres on Robinson's Cr. waters of Haw R.; Peter Stroud, Robt. Marsh: CC.

Murray, Benjamin   Warrant   18 June 1761
700 acres in forks betwixt Flatt R. & Deep Cr., begin on James Blakley's line, includes his own improvements.
"This property Justly & Legally made over of the within warrant from Benjamin Morrow to John Tharp in prescence of John Lea, Jas Blakley"
Deed 6 Dec 1761

Blackley, James   Warrant   18 June 1761
700 acres on Deep Cr., waters of Flatt R. Begin on John Thomas' line.
Surveyed 20 Oct 1761
Deed 6 Dec 1761

Shepherd, Andrew   Survey   18 June 1761
315 acres on big Lick Cr., west side Cape Fair R., adjoins William Hinton on Earl Granville's line; Woolrick Keesy: CB.

Binum, Luke   Warrant   23 June 1761
700 acres on Newhope Cr. begin at John Faulconers line.
Surveyed 24 Oct 1761

Boyd, John   Survey   23 June 1761
300 acres on south side Deep R., begin at Duncan Bohannon; Joseph Fuller, John Fuller: CC.

Lantrop, Thomas   Survey   26 June 1761
130 acres on north side Rocky R.; Thos. Copeland, Nehemiah Posey: CC.

Copeland, Thomas   Survey   26 June 1761
225 acres on Richland Cr. waters of Rocky R.;
Nehemiah Posey, Jeremiah Leper: CC.

Salling, Geo. Adam   Survey   30 June 1761
470 acres on Rocky R.; Charl's Sinklar, Wm Lasey: CB.

Martin, Zachariah, Jr. Survey   3 July 1761
585 acres on Dry Cr.; Ellathan Davis, John Crow: CC.
Deed 6 Dec 1761

Lane, Richard   Warrant   13 July 1761
700 acres on both sides Country Line Cr., joins
Joseph Dolittle & Thomas Laxton.
Surveyed 11 Jan 1762
Deed 6 Mar 1762

White, Woolrick   Warrant   14 July 1761
700 acres on south side Rocky R., joins Capt.
Zachariah Martin, includes his own improvements.
Surveyed 5 Jan 1762

Harvey, William   Survey   17 July 1761
414 acres on the Main south fork of Richland Cr.
waters of Deep R.; Paul Paulson, Michael Harvey: CC.

Welborn, Wm., Junr.   Survey   18 July 1761
375 acres on McEntires Cr., waters of Deep R.;
Isaac Starns, Charles Cagle: CB.

Graves, Thomas   Warrant   22 July 1761
700 acres on Deep R. begin on William Searcy upper
line, includes James Graves' & his own improvements.
Surveyed 10 Dec 1761

McGowen, James, Jr.   Warrant   27 July 1761
700 acres on McGowen's Cr. waters of Enoe, joins
Minnis & Mitchel.
Deed 6 Mar 1762

Haley, David   Survey   29 July 1761
421 acres on ridge between Country Line Cr. &
Rattlesnake Cr.; John Oaks, Robt. Whitton: SCC.

Lacey, William   Warrant   4 Aug 1761
700 acres on Laceys Cr. waters of Rocky R., includes his own, Duckworth & Webb improvements.
Surveyed 24 Nov 1761

Barker, Nicholas   Warrant   4 Aug 1761
700 acres on Painter Creek the waters of Richland
Creek the waters of Deep R., begin about a mile
above the mouth of Painter Cr.
Surveyed 3 Dec 1761

Nelson, Moses   Warrant   4 Aug 1761
700 acres on Alder Br. waters of Rocky R., includes his improvements.
Surveyed 23 Nov 1761

Doane, John   Warrant   4 Aug 1761
700 acres on a branch of Caine Cr., joins Anthony
Chamnes & Simon Dixon, where he now lives.
Surveyed 21 Nov 1761

Young, Ruben   Warrant   6 Aug 1761
700 acres on Buffelow Cr. waters of Little R.,
includes place he now lives on.
Surveyed 27 Jan 1762
Deed 6 Mar 1762

Hogg, Gideon   Survey   13 Aug 1761
135 acres on Greens Cr. of Dan R., on provence
line; Major Lea, Jas Watkins: SCC.

Talbert, James   Survey   14 Aug 1761
649 acres on the Rich-land-creek of Hicoe, joins
Jas. Anderson, sd Talbert, Bankson; John Talbert,
Thos Anderson: SCC.

Trolinger, Adam   Warrant   18 Aug 1761
700 acres on south side Haw R., includes plantation he now lives on.
Surveyed 16 Sept 1761
Deed 6 Dec 1761

Pitts, John   Warrant   20 Aug 1761
700 acres on north fork of White Oak a br. of New
Hope, about a half mile from the main cr.
Surveyed 21 Oct 1761(?)

Smith, John   Entry   22 Aug 1761
700 acres on Crabtree Cr. (Empty Shuck).

Harris, Thompson   Warrant   24 Aug 1761
700 acres on Pruitts Fork of Hogans Cr.
Surveyed 20 Jan 1762
Deed 6 Mar 1762

Davis, Adam   Survey   25 Aug 1761
300 acres on the trading path the west side of Haw
R., joins Philip and McCullochs; Wm Hopkins, Chas
(Torn): CC.

Bray, Henry   Warrant   25 Aug 1761
700 acres on south br of Rocky R. begin near the

head of a spring on the west side of the land including his own improvements & those of Henry Switzer.
Surveyed 26 Nov 1761

Phillips, David, Senr. Warrant 2 Sept 1761
700 acres on Nelsons Run waters of Haw R., includes his own, David Phillips, Jr., & Jesse Phillips improvements.
Surveyed 27 Feb 1762

Cheyney, Francis Warrant 3 Sept 1761
700 acres on the north fork of Richland Cr. waters of Deep R., includes his own improvements.
Surveyed 3 Dec 1761

O'Daniel (Adaniel), John, Jr. Warrant 5 Sept 1761
700 acres on waters of Back Cr. waters of Haw R., includes plantation William Adaniel now lives on.
"Void by Robt Tate's Entry & the Money Returned"

Vaughn, Daniel by Thomas Hart Entry 9 Sept 1761
700 acres on Pruitts Fk. of Hogans Cr., joins Thompson Harris, includes his own improvements.

Vaughn, David Warrant 9 Sept 1761
700 acres on pruitts Fk. of Hogans Cr., joins Thompson Harris, includes his own improvements.
Surveyed 9 Feb 1762
Deed 6 Mar 1762

Alexander, Thomas Entry 12 Sept 1761
700 acres on south fork of Rocky River, includes his own improvements, signed Thomas "T" Alexander.

Alexander, Thomas Warraant 12 Sept 1761
700 acres on South Fork of Rocky River, includes his own improvements.
Surveyed 23 Nov 1761

Straughan, Richard Entry 15 Sept 1761
700 acres on Caine island Creek, waters of Haw, includes Clanton's Folley, signed with a mark.

Eason, Joshua Entry 16 Sept 1761
700 acres on both sides Benjamin Bowlings Cr., waters of New Hope, begin at John King's corner, signed with a mark.

Fulkerson, James Entry 18 Sept 1761
700 acres on north side of Hico, on head of Watery Br., includes the fork of the roads & a logg meeting house.

Ogle, Harculus Entry 21 Sept 1761
700 acres on south side Deep R., opposite mouth of Sandy Cr., includes his own improvements, signed with a mark.

Corley, Robert Entry 2 Oct 1761
700 acres on Robeson's Cr., waters of Haw R., includes his own improvements.

Akin, Joseph Entry 3 Oct 1761
700 acres on Dann R., begin at south of Haywoods Br.

Murray, Thomas Entry 5 Oct 1761
700 acres on waters of Enoe, joins Synnott & White, includes Brannon's improvements, entry made by Giden (Gideon) Lincicum (Lincecum) for Murray.

Moore, David Survey 12 oct 1761
168 acres on Forest Cr. of Little R., joins Gaddis, Anglen; Jas. Anglen, Jno Thomas: SCC.

Presnall, Jacob Warrant 23 Oct 1761
700 acres on a br. of Richland Cr. waters of Deep R., includes his improvements.
"Void by Benjn Ellis Warrant & the money Returned"

Bennett, Joseph Entry 23 Oct 1761
Signed: Jos. Barnett
700 acres on Castle Cr., waters of Hico, adj. lines of Big Robert McFarland & John Hurley.

Barr. James Entry 29 Oct 1761
700 acres on west side of Meho R., a fork of Dan R., includes improvements bought of Richard Simson joining Johnston King.

Norton, Stephen Warrant 3 Nov 1761
700 acres on Mayho Cr., adjoins Donaldson & Giles.
"No Land to be found, Being taken on elder warrant of John Pryor Esq."

Webb, James by John Lea Entry 4 Nov 1761
700 acres in fork of Mayho Cr., joins John Giles.

Harden, Benjamin Entry 4 Nov 1761
700 acres on Haw R. begin on Widow Carruther's line, includes his own & George Smith's improvements, signed with a mark.

Doolittle, Joseph Entry 4 Nov 1761
700 acres on Woolf island Cr., begin on Burd's line.

Lloyd, Thomas, Esq. Entry 5 Nov 1761
700 acres on north side Haw R., on Caine Cr.

Martin, Zachariah, Capt.　　Entry　　　　　7 Nov 1761
　　700 acres on Arnold's Cr. waters of Rocky R.,
　　joins Timothy Terril and Soloman Terril.

Mackie, Watson & Co.　　Entry　　　　　9 Nov 1761
　　700 acres on south side Capfair R., joins survey
　　of Campbell.

Hughes, Charles　　　Entry　　　　　12 Nov 1761
　　700 acres begin on the third fork from the mouth
　　of the said creek (on Stoney Cr.)

Sample, James by Robert Tate　Entry　　　20 Nov 1761
　　700 acres on Back Cr., Haw R., includes said
　　Tate's improvements, signed with a mark.

West, Richard by John Bowie　Entry　　　5 Dec 1761
　　700 acres on south side Haw R., includes Thomas
　　North, Cornelius Roe & William Hooker's improve-
　　ments.

Goodbread, Philip　　　Entry　　　　　12 Dec 1761
　　700 acres on Back Cr., waters of Haw R., includes
　　his improvements, signed with a mark.

Aldridge, Nathaniel by James Watson　Entry　19 Dec 1761
　　700 acres onn Flat R., adjoins Thomas Robinson's
　　line.

Armfield, Jacob by James Watson　　Entry　21 Dec 1761
　　700 acres on mouth of the Reedy Br. of Brush Cr.,
　　waters of Deep R., near Cox's Road.

Nicholson, James by James Watson　Entry　21 Dec 1761
　　700 acres on a br. of Sandy Cr., waters of Deep
　　R., joins Herman Husband, includes plantation
　　where Lowe & Fulsum now live.

Parker, Samuell, by Joseph Barbee　Entry　4 Jan 1762
　　700 acres on Prices Cr., waters of New Hope,
　　includes his own improvements.

Hart, Nathaniel, by James Watson　Entry　6 Jan 1762
　　700 acres on Natts Fork of Country Line Cr. near
　　George Boid.

Tomerlinson, John　　　Entry　　　　6 Jan 1762
　　700 acres on south side Deep R., begin below mouth
　　of Little Buffelow Cr., signed with a mark.

Ray, James　　　　　Entry　　　　　12 Jan 1762
　　700 acres on Little Cr. of Robesons Cr., waters of
　　Haw R., begin at mouth of the Little Cr., joins
　　William Petty, signed with a mark.

Barns, Jacob by Elisha Hunter　Entry　　13 Jan 1762
　　700 acres on Bear Cr., waters of Rocky R.

Lathem, James by James Watson　Entry　　14 Jan 1762
　　700 acres on Fork Cr., waters of Deep R. about 1/2
　　mile above Enoch Spink's line.

Beezly, Henry by James Watson　Entry　　14 Jan 1762
　　700 acres in fork of Obe's Cr., waters of New Hope.

Allison, James by James Watson　Entry　　14 Jan 1762
　　700 acres on Back Cr., waters of Haw R., Begin
　　about 1/4 mile above fork of Staggs Cr. & Back Cr.

Brantley, John, Jr. by James Watson　Entry　15 Jan 1762
　　700 acres on both sides of Rocky R., includes
　　plantation where Thomas Lantrop formerly lived.

Hamelton, Ninean Bell by James Watson
　　　　　　　　　　, Entry　　　　18 Jan 1762
　　700 acres on a br. of the head of Rocky R., above
　　Thomas Alexander including the Turkey Thicket.

Dixon, Soloman　　　Warrant　　　　27 Jan 1762
　　700 acres on Haw R. & Terrils Cr. "No land to be
　　found is being taken by Robt. Cates - John Lea."
　　"Entry Money Returned - by - Jas Watson"

Dixon, Soloman by James Watson　Entry　　27 Jan 1762
　　700 acres on Haw R. & Terrils Cr.

Dixon, Joseph by James Watson　Entry　　27 Jan 1762
　　700 acres on Tick Cr., waters of Rocky R., joins
　　John May, includes Benjn Williams' improvements.

Whitehead, Amos by James Watson　Entry　　28 Jan 1762
　　700 acres on Seven Mile Cr., waters of Enoe, begin
　　at mouth of Long Br., includes Hooper's Cabin.

Walker, Moses by James Watson　Entry　　28 Jan 1762
　　700 acres on a br. of Mayho, includes improvements
　　that Burk lived on.

Barbe, Joseph　　　Entry　　　　　1 Feb 1762
　　(Very Fragile) Old Field & Bolins Cr. of New Hope.

George, David, Jr.　　Warrant　　　　1 Feb 1762
　　700 acres on the hicory Mountain, includes Richard
　　Copelands improvements. "No land to be found,
　　being relapsed in favour to Mr. Copeland. Entry
　　Money Returned by - Jas. Watson."

Powell, Nathaniel by James Watson　Entry　1 Feb 1762
　　700 acres on Deep R., begin at Line Cr., place
　　where Nipper now lives.

Jones, Henry by James Watson   Entry   1 Feb 1762
    700 acres on Elebys Cr., joins Robert Clenton.

Terry, Stephen by James Watson   Entry   2 Feb 1762
    700 acres on Pruitts Fork of Hogans Cr., a 1/2 mile above David Vahns line.

Rhodes, John by James Watson   Entry   2 Feb 1762
    700 acres on Deep R., begin at his own line.

Copeland, Nicholas, Junr., by James Watson
                                    Entry   3 Feb 1762
    700 acres on Great Cr., waters of Rocky R., below Round topt Mountain, including Hams folly.

Clenton, Charles, by Jas Watson   Entry   3 Feb 1762
    700 acres on Robeson's Cr waters of Haw, joins William Petty's line.

Clenton, Charles   Warrant   3 Feb 1762
    700 acres on Robeson's Cr, waters of Haw, joins William Petty
    "No Land to be found, being taken by a former Warrant of his Own - signed John Lea."

McGee, John by James Watson   Entry   3 Feb 1762
    700 acres on a br. of Sandy Cr., waters of Deep R., both sides of the western (Torn), includes Hercules Ogles Cabin.

Doaks, John by James Watson   Entry   8 Feb 1762
    700 acres On Alaman(Torn) including the place called the B(Torn). On reverse "On Alamans Haw River."

Parson, Thomas by James Watson   Entry   8 Feb 1762
    700 acres on Dials Creek, waters of Flatt R., joins James Horton.

Clenton, Edward by James Watson   Entry   14 Feb 1762
    700 acres on Drt Creek, waters of Haw R., includes Blosingam's improvements.

Julian, John   Entry   16 Feb 1762
    700 acres on Rush Creek, waters of Deep R.

Youngblood, Jacob by James Watson   Entry   16 Feb 1762
    700 acres on south fork of Rocky R., adjoins George Hobson, Jr., includes his own & Jonathon William's improvements.

Julian, Isaac by James Watson   Entry   16 Feb 1762
    700 acres on mouth of Polecat Cr., waters of Deep R., near Gabriel Freeman, includes his improvements.

Barber, William   Entry   17 Feb 1762
    (Very Fragile, most of writing gone) Indian Cr. of Deep R.

Linch, John by James Watson   Entry   18 Feb 1762
    700 acres between Staggs Cr. & Back Cr., waters of Haw R., includes Zachary Cadles improvements.

Thompson, Robert by James Watson   Entry   23 Feb 1762
    700 acres on Camp Cr., waters of Flatt R.

Thompson, Robert by Thomas Hart   Entry   23 Feb 1762
    700 acres on Flatt R., begin on James Watson's line, adjoins John Brown's line.

Thompson, Robert by Thos. Hart   Entry   23 Feb 1762
    700 acres on Little Cr., waters of Flatt R., below Gibsons Path.

Whitton, Thomas by James Watson   Entry   1 Mar 1762
    700 acres on Country Line Cr., includes his improvements.

Reed, William, Esq. by James Watson Entry   1 Mar 1762
    700 acres on south side Rambo's Br. waters of Hico, includes Branches of the Bald Branch.

Husband, Herman by James Watson   Entry   2 Mar 1762
    700 acres on Deep R., adjoins his own & Jesse Holingsworth's lines.

Husband, Herman   Entry   2 Mar 1762
    700 acres on Tick Cr. waters of Rocky R. on both sides of Hermans Road, signed by Jas. Watson.

Ratcliif, Joel   Entry   4 Mar 1762
    700 acres on the middle fork of the third fork of New Hope, joins Jackson Rhodes.

Boilston, William   Entry   12 Mar 1762
    700 acres on Harpers Br., waters of Rocky R., Includes his own & John McDaniels improvements, signed by a mark.

Davis, James by James Kendrick   Entry   15 Mar 1762
    700 acres on both sides of Deep R., joins Churton's & Dowdy's lines.

Morgan, Mark   Entry   20 Mar 1762
    700 acres on Cubb Cr. of New Hope, includes James Rigsby's improvements.

Morgan, Mark   Entry   20 Mar 1762
    700 acres on waters of Morgans Cr., begin above John Rigsbys improvements including the Chappel &

the Three Springs.

Morgan, Mark　　　　Entry　　　　20 Mar 1762
700 acres on Cubb Cr. waters of New Hope between his former lines.

Morgan, Mark　　　　Entry　　　　20 Mar 1762
700 acres on New Hope Cr., begin below the Beaver Ponds on his own line.

Stubblefield, John　Entry　　　　20 Mar 1762
700 acres on Reedy Fork of Hogans Cr., joins his own & Robt. Jone's line, includes Jarret's improvements, signed with a mark.

Morgan, Mark　　　　Warrant　　　20 Mar 1762
700 acres on waters of Morgans & Rolins Cr., begin above John Rigby's improvements, includes the Chappel & the 3 Springs.

King, Thomas　　　　Entry　　　　22 Mar 1762
700 acres on Matt Couches Cr., waters of Enoe, joins Matt Couch.

Hadley, Jerimiah　　Entry　　　　22 Mar 1762
700 acres on Nicks Cr. waters of Rocky R., includes improvement Elijah Teague lives on.

Bowie, James　　　　Entry　　　　22 Mar 1762
700 acres on Seven Mile Cr., waters of Enoe, adj. James Couch.

Parker, Richard, Esq.　Entry　　　30 Mar 1762
700 acres on Bush Cr., waters of New Hope, joins his own line & includes James Ewing's improvements.

Barbe, John, Senr.　Entry　　　　1 Apr 1762
700 acres on NE Br. of New Hope, begin near the lick br. above George Herrendon & Bennett's lines.

Lea, Zachariah by John Lea　Entry　　1 Apr 1762
(Very Fragile & Torn) ...Hico including his own improvements, Rushing Br. of South Hico.

Mullis, John　　　　Entry　　　　12 Apr 1762
700 acres on Robeson's Cr., waters of Haw R., includes his improvements.

Leavens, Nicholas Perkins　Entry　　17 Apr 1762
700 acres on Hosleys Cr., waters of Deep R.

Bell, Thomas　　　　Assignment　　20 Apr 1762
700 acres on branch of Bear Swp to Arthur Williams.

Teague, Edward, Junr. by Edward Teague Sr.
　　　　　　　　　　Entry　　　　27 Apr 1762
700 acres on waters of Rocky R., joins Edward Teague, Senr.

Davis, David　　　　Entry　　　　3 May 1762
700 acres on Stinking Cr., waters of Haw R., includes Mullis & Johnstons improvements, signed by mark.

Bray, Henry, Jr.　　Warrant　　　4 May 1762
700 acres on Brush Cr., waters of Deep R., includes Taylor's improvements.

Braizier, Thomas by John Pyle　Entry　4 May 1762
700 acres on Terrils Cr., waters of Haw R.

Banks, David by Jas. Watson　Entry　5 May 1762
700 acres on Terrils Cr., waters of Haw R.

Brewer, Oliver by Henry Brewer　Entry　5 May 1762
700 acres on Little prong of Terrels Cr., waters of Haw R., includes Saplin Level. Signed with mark.

Dunagan, Thomas. Junr.　Entry　　　10 May 1762
700 acres on Little R., joins Wm Churton & John Barney.

Whitehead, Robert　Warrant　　　21 May 1762
700 acres on Lick Br. Haw R., includes his own improvements.

McVey, Daniel　　　Warrant　　　2 Aug 1762
William Berry (interlined)
700 acres on south side Caine Cr., includes McVey's improvements.
"The above was Entered by William Berry & by Berry's consent to be Returned in Daniel McVey's name as Mr. Churton & Mr. Lea informed me - Jas Watson - John Lea Witness to the agreement between Berry & McVey."

Cury, Nathaniel　　Warrant　　　26 Aug 1762
700 acres on both sides of Whit Oak Swamp, includes three small improvements where David Marler formerly lived.
Deed 1 Apr 1763

Smith, John　　　　Warrant　　　11 Sept 1762
700 acres on south fork of Little Rock Cr. waters of Alamance, includes his improvements.
"Recd in this Office 4 Dec 1763"

King, John　　　　Warrant　　　9 Oct 1762

700 acres on the Reedy Fork of Haw R. joins
Middleton Brashear.
Surveyed 5 June 1763

Day, John   Warrant   9 Oct 1762
700 acres on Robesons Cr. of Haw R., includes
William Lotts improvements.
Surveyed 9 Mar 17__

Mitchel, Robert   Warrant   9 Oct 1762
700 acres on waters of Alamans, joins David Brown.
"N B William Brown will attend the Surveyor on
notice given" (interlined)

Martin, Zachariah   Warrant   12 Oct 1762
700 acres on Meadow Cr. of Rocky R., joins his own
& Peter Youngblood's land.
Surveyed 12 Mar 1763

Lindly, James   Warrant   14 Oct 1762
700 acres on Cane Cr., south side Haw R., includes
his own & Mary Long's improvements.

Boon, Jacob   Warrant   19 Oct 1762
700 acres on Cedar Cr., waters of Alamans, adj.
McCulloch's line, includes Conrad Nave's improvements.
"The above warrant Altered from John Whitman to
Jacob Boon per agreement Lodged with - Jas Watson"

Aven, Joseph   Warrant   21 Oct 1762
700 acres on Shaddock's Creek of Haw R.
Surveyed 23 Feb 1763

Stewart, John   Warrant   22 Oct 1762
700 acres in the fork of Haw & Deep R., joins
William Marsh.
Surveyed 20 Apr 1763

Gregg, Jacob   Warrant   27 Oct 1762
700 acres on Milstone Cr. Deep R. begin about a
mile east of Herman Cox's line.
Surveyed 27 Apr 1763

Kell, Thomas   Warrant   29 Oct 1762
700 acres on waters of Little R. joins Willm.
Mebane & Patrick Rutherford.
Surveyed 20 Apr 1763

Matthews, George   Warrant   2 Nov 1762
700 acres on Caine Cr. south side Haw R., joins
Laughlone & Brooks, includes his own improvements.
Surveyed 23 Apr 1763

Perkins, Peter   Warrant   5 Nov 1762
700 acres on waters of Enoe, joins James McGowan,
Jr.
Surveyed 2 May 1763

Phillips, John   Warrant   20 Nov 1762
700 acres on Haw R., joins William Phillips & Adam
Trolinger.

Whitehead, Robert   Survey   21 Nov 1762
303 acres on Lick Br. of Haw R.; Robert Whitehead,
Nathan Carter CC. 3 copies.

Robertson, John   Warrant   2 Dec 1762
700 acres on Haw R., begin near mouth of Fishing
Cr., includes Church's improvements.
Surveyed 27 May 1763

Denny, Zachariah   Warrant   2 Dec 1762
700 acres on the Broad Br. of Mayo Cr. adjoins the
county line begin on Robert Jones Cor.
Surveyed 15 May 1763

Walker, John   Warrant   9 Dec 1762
700 acres on a branch of County Line Cr., includes
Thomas Cunningham's improvements.
Surveyed 3 June 1763

Holsenbeck, Derrick   Warrant   11 Dec 1762
700 acres on Grices' Cr., Hico, joins David Mitchell.
Surveyed 3 June 1763

Stewart, Samuel   Warrant   12 Dec 1762
700 acres on Terral's Cr., Haw R.
Surveyed 10 June 1763

Teague, Abraham   Warrant   13 Dec 1762
700 acres on waters of Dry Cr. Haw R., includes
his and Moses Teague's improvements.
Surveyed 10 June 1763

Cole, John   Warrant   14 Dec 1762
(Coole)
700 acres on White Oak Cr., waters of Buckhorn,
adj. John Utley's line.
Surveyed 9 June 1763

Armstrong, John   Warrant   20 Dec 1762
700 acres on middle fork of Little River, joins
his own and Nathl Walton's lines.
Surveyed 12 June 1763

Elliman, John   Warrant   20 Dec 1762
700 acres on the north fork of Little R., adjoins
his own and Nathaniel Watson's lines.

Surveyed 12 June 1763

Walker, John   Warrant   21 Dec 1762
700 acres on the head of Hogan's Cr., on both sides the path leading from Bird's to Pain's.
Surveyed 17 June 1763

Mangum, Arthur   Warrant   27 Dec 1762
700 acres on both sides Flatte R., joins Thomas Gibson.
Surveyed 12 June 1763

Hart, Thomas   Warrant   30 Dec 1762
700 acres on forks of Jordan Cr., on both sides Cantrels Path & the New Cut Road.
Surveyed 26 June 1763

Holeday, Henry   Warrant   30 Dec 1762
700 acres on Caine Cr. south side Haw R., joins Francis Jones & Thos. Lindley.

Watson, James, Jr.   Warrant   3 Jan 1763
700 acres in fork of Jordans Cr. & Stoney Cr., on both sides Stoney Cr.
Surveyed 27 June 1763

Reed, William   Warrant   3 Jan 1763
700 acres on Seven Mile Cr. waters of Enoe R., joins James Watson's line.
Surveyed 6 June 1763

Bredin, Robert   Warrant   17 Jan 1763
700 acres on N Buffelow, adj. George Hambellon's line, includes Alexr Bredin's improvements.
Surveyed 13 July 1763

Davis, Benjamin   Warrant   17 Jan 1763
700 acres on Collins's Cr. Haw R., joins Jonathon Harden.
Surveyed 12 July 1763

Harrelson, Burges   Warrant   17 Jan 1763
700 acres on Marlow's Cr. waters of Hico, joins Willm Stone, Edwd Chambers & Burgess Harrelson.
Surveyed 12 July 1763

Laughlan, Richard   Warrant   19 Jan 1763
700 acres on Marys Cr Haw R. includes his own improvements.

Phillips, John   Survey   20 Jan 1763
683 acres on west side Haw R., joins Trollenger, Sharp; Thomas Sharp, Ginnins Thompson: CC. 3 copies

Cooper, Isaac   Warrant   22 Jan 1763
700 acres on Buckhorn Cr, includes his own improvements
Surveyed 15 July 1763

Linen, Hugh   Survey   23 Jan 1763
700 acres on waters of Cain Creek of Haw R., joins John Pile; William Mcforson, John Orman: SCC. "Daniel McVey" is the name on the plat. Assignment of Daniel McVey to Hugh Linen, tract on south side Cain Cr., wit.: Thomas Lindley, William Lindley, dated 7 Feb 1764. 3 copies of survey.

Carr, David   Warrant   1 Feb 1763
700 acres on S. Buffelow, adj. John McDaniel.
Surveyed 20 July 1763

Husband, Herman   Warrant   1 Feb 1763
700 acres on Brush Cr. of Deep R. includes James Hawkins improv.
Surveyed 27 July 1763

Forbus, Arthur   Warrant   1 Feb 1763
700 acres on Burch Cr. Haw R., joins William Wiley, includes Thomas Morgan's improvements.
Surveyed 20 July 1763

Boyd, John, Jr.   Warrant   1 Feb 1763
700 acres on Great Troublesome including his own improvements.
Surveyed 27 July 1763

Oldham, James   Warrant   1 Feb 1763
700 acres on Piney Br. Haw R., includes Thos. Church's improvements.
Surveyed 29 Apr 1763.

Watson, James   Warrant   1 Feb 1763
700 acres on Elebys Cr., joins James Bowie, includes Stephen Merit's improvements. Entered by James Bowie & conveyed to James Watson.
Surveyed 23 July 1763

Shepherd, Andrew   Warrant   1 Feb 1763
700 acres on Bush Cr. Cap Fear R., begin on sd Granville's line, includes Ward's & Walker's improvements.
Surveyed 26 July 1763

Sutherland, Mordecai   Warrant   1 Feb 1763
700 acres on Cub islanbd Cr. of Enoe R., includes William Manning's improvements.
Surveyed 24 July 1763

Camp, Edward   Warrant   2 Feb 1763
700 acres on the Double Creeks waters of Hico at

Sarratts old line.
Surveyed 29 July 1763

Montgomery, William   Warrant   2 Feb 1763
700 acres on Buckhorn Br. waters of Little R., joins John Burney & Wm Churton.
Surveyed 18 July 1763

Rutherford, Patrick   Warrant   14 Feb 1763
700 acres on branches of Lick Cr., Flatt R., on south side Robert Berry.
Surveyed 8 Aug 1763

Mateer, William   Warrant   14 Feb 1763
700 acres on Thonody's Cr. of Haw R., joins Vendorgrove Thonody (Konody).
Surveyed 12 July 1763

Boon, Jacob   Survey   19 Feb 1763
482 acres, "at Alleman of Haw R.", adj. McCulloch's line; Peter Baker, Conrad Strader: CB. 3 copies.

Avin, Joseph   Survey   21 Feb 1763
350 acres on Shaddock Cr, Haw R.; Elisha Cane, Bracket Wood: CB.

Graves, Thomas   Warrant   21 Feb 1763
700 acres, joins Peter Youngblood on waters of Rocky R.
Surveyed 20 July 1763

Griffen, Jonas   Warrant   22 Feb 1763
700 acres on Flatt R., joins John Brown, John Carrington.
Surveyed 15 Aug 1763
"To Wm Jones"
Includes assignment by Griffen - illegible - dated 1764

Latta, James   Warrant   22 Feb 1763
700 acres on waters of Eno, joins his own line.
Surveyed 23 July 1763

Avin, Joseph   Survey   23 Feb 1763
350 acres on Shaddock's Creek; Elisha Cane, Bracket Wood: SCC. 3 copies

Brooks, Robert, Sr.   Warrant   1 Mar 1763
700 acres on a branch of Mayo, joins Maho.
Surveyed 1 Aug 1763

McPherson, William   Warrant   1 Mar 1763
700 acres on waters of Caine Cr., Haw R., joins Jno Piles.
Surveyed 18 Sept 1763

McPherson, William   Warrant   1 Mar 1763
700 acres on waters of Cain Cr. of Haw R., joins James Moon.
Surveyed 18 Sept. 1763

Stout, Peter   Warrant   1 Mar 1763
700 acres on Reedy Br. of Caine Cr. Haw R., joins his line.
Surveyed 26 Aug 1763.

Poplin, George   Survey   1 Mar 1763
700 acres on Beare Cr. of Rocky R., joins Ragsdale; Jas. Willet, Jno. Miles: SCC. 2 copies

Griffen, William   Warrant   10 Mar 1763
700 acres on a br. of Morgan's Cr., New Hope, near the Round Mountain.
Surveyed 5 Sept 1763

Smith, John   Survey   10 Mar 1763
700 acres on Rock Cr. of Haw R., joins McCullock; Peter Lawrence, Wm Forbush: CC. 3 copies

Lloyd, Frederick   Warrant   10 Mar 1763
700 acres on head of Colin's Cr., including head of Morgans Cr.
Surveyed 5 Sept 1763

Martin, Zachariah   Survey   12 Mar 1763
503 acres on Meadow Cr. of Rocky R., joins Joab Brooks, Youngblood; Jas. Emmerson, Jno Youngblood: SCC. 3 copies.

Jones, Stephen   Warrant   21 Mar 1763
700 acres on a br. of Sandy Cr.
Surveyed 15 Sept 1763

Justice, James   Warrant   21 Mar 1763
700 acres on Deep Cr, Flatt R., including Rich Hill & improvements.
Surveyed 15 Aug 1763

Hart, Thomas   Warrant   22 Mar 1763
700 acres on ridge between Country Line Cr. & Haw R., both sides of the new Cutt Road.
Surveyed 20 Sept 1763

Tapley, Hosea   Warrant   22 Mar 1763
700 acres on waters of north fork of Flatt R., joins his own line.
Surveyed 15 Sept 1763

Beemer, Peter   Warrant   30 Mar 1763

700 acres on west fork of Double Cr., waters of South Hico.
Surveyed 10 Sept 1761
Deed 6 Dec 1761

Grave, John　　　　Warrant　　　　4 Apr 1763
700 acres on Benaja Cr. of Country Line, includes William Wilson's improvements.
Surveyed 10 Sept 1763

Hart, Thomas　　　　Warrant　　　　5 Apr 1763
700 acres on waters of Haw R. & Country Line Cr., joins Aaron Pinson.
Surveyed 3 Oct 1763
Returned 1 Jan 1765

Mitchel, Robert　　　Survey　　　　8 Apr 1763
488 acres on Allamance of Haw R., joins Andrew Findley, David Brown; David Brown, John Michal: SCC. 3 copies

Linley, James　　　　Survey　　　　15 Apr 1763
665 acres on Cane Cr. of Haw R.; Joseph Richason, Joseph Wright: SCC. 2 copies.

Kell, Thos　　　　Survey　　　　20 Apr 1763
427 acres on waters of Little R., joins Mebane, Rutherford; Jno Murdoc, Jno Elliman: SCC. 3 copies

Stewart, John　　　　Survey　　　　20 Apr 1763
206 acres on waters of Haw R., joins Martin, Marsh, Brooks; Robt Marsh, Jas. Stewart: SCC. 2 copies.

Norton, Edward　　　Survey　　　　23 Apr 1763
586 acres on Sandy Cr. of Deep R., joins Herman Husband, McGee; Ed McCain, Richd Norton: SCC. 3 copies

Matthews, George　　Survey　　　　23 Apr 1763
697 acres on Cain Cr. of Haw R., joins Laughlin, Brooks; Joel Brooks, Jas. Brooks: SCC. 3 copies

Gregg, Jacob　　　　Survey　　　　27 Apr 1763
670 acres on Millstone Cr of Deep R.; Nich Barker, Saml Barker: SCC. 3 copies

Oldham, James　　　Survey　　　　29 Apr 1763
180 acres on north side Haw R., joins Robt. Wells; Robt. Wells, Jessey Oldham: SCC. 2 copies

Boyd, William　　　　Warrant　　　　2 May 1763
700 acres on Little Troublesome Cr. of Haw R. "Betwixt John Boids Lines."
Surveyed 1 Nov 1763

Arrengton, Charles　Warrant　　　　2 May 1763
700 acres on Lick Creek Capfear River, begin on Drury Mim's line.
Surveyed 27 Oct 1763.

Rhodes, William　　Warrant　　　　3 May 1763
700 acres on waters of New Hope, joins William Pickett's upper line.
Surveyed 25 Oct 1763

Shepherd, Andrew　　Warrant　　　　5 May 1763
700 acres on west side Cap Fear R., includes place called the Red Land.
Surveyed 3 Nov 1763

Harrison, William　Warrant　　　　13 May 1763
700 acres on Little Troublesome Creek of Haw R., includes his own improvements.
Surveyed 10 Nov 1763

Denny, Zach.　　　Survey　　　　15 May 1763
207 acres on Broad Br. of Mayo, on Province line; Wm Brooks, Wm Price: SCC. 3 copies

Hollan, James　　　Survey　　　　24 May 1763
682 acres in Cumberland & Orange Counties on both sides Utleys Cr., near Barkers Mill; John Cole, (Torn)ultman: CB.

Robinson, John　　　Survey　　　　27 May 1763
700 acres on Fishing Cr. & Haw R.; Hugh Porter, Charles Howe: SCC. 3 copies.

McFarlan, John　　　Warrant　　　　31 May 1763
700 acres on Tents Cr. of Hico, includes his son's improvements.
Surveyed 30 Oct 1763

Holsenpack, Derick　Survey　　　　3 June 1763
397 acres on waters of S. Hicoe, joins Thos. Williams, Jno Rainey, Robt Carson: SCC. 3 copies

King, John　　　　Survey　　　　5 June 1763
655 acres on Reedy Fork of Haw R., joins Hugh Porter; Phillip Brashear, Ralph Shaw: CC. 3 copies

Reed, William　　　Survey　　　　6 June 1763
160 acres on Seven Mile Cr., joins James Watson; James Watson, Joseph Bird: SCC. 3 copies.

Teague, Abraham　　Survey　　　　10 June 1763
675 acres on waters of Dry Cr. of Haw R.; Jas McClester, Walter Ashmore: SCC. 3 copies.

Armstrong, John　　Survey　　　　12 June 1763

412 acres on waters of Little R., joins his own and Nathl Walton's lines; Jno Ellimon, Enos Ellimon: SCC. 3 copies

Mangum, Arthur   Survey   12 June 1763
357 acres on Flatt R., joins Jno Dunnagin, Thos. Gibson; Robt. Thomson, Jno Collins: SCC. 2 copies.

Elliman. John   Survey   12 June 1763
92 acres on waters of Little R., joins his own line; Pautrick Rotherford, Enos Elliman: SCC. 3 copies

Walker, John   Survey   17 June 1763
210 acres on the head of Hogan Cr. of Dan R.; Jas Nichols, Wm Mateer: SCC. 3 copies.

Hollada (Holada), Henry Survey   22 June 1763
319 acres on Cain Cr. of Haw R., joins Francis Jones, Hollensworth; Joseph Richarson, Joseph Wheant: SCC. 3 copies

Hart, Thomas   Survey   26 June 1763
400 acres on Jordans Cr. of Haw R.; Geo. Elmore, Thos Barnes: SCC. 3 copies

Watson, James, Jr.   Survey   27 June 1763
291 acres on fork of Stoney Cr. & Jordans Cr. of Haw R.; Soloman West, Robt. Tate: SCC. 2 copies.

Harrelson, Burges   Survey   12 July 1763
180 acres on Marlows Cr. of Hicoe, joins Stone, Paul Harrelson,; Paul Harrelson, Elisha Harrelson: SCC . 3 copies

Mateer, William   Survey   12 July 1763
220 acres on Giles Cr. of Haw R., joins Giles Tillet; Jas. Shirret, Jno Walker: SCC. 3 copies

Mateer, William   Survey   12 July 1763
384 acres on Kennidays Cr. of Haw R., joins Vandegrove, Kenniday; Jas. Stirret, Jno Walker: SCC. 3 copies.

Davis, Benjamin   Survey   12 July 1763
410 acres on Collins's Cr of Haw R., joins Harden; Jno Buckner, Wm Stroud: SCC. 3 copies

Breeding, Robert   Survey   13 July 1763
310 acres on waters of No. Buffaloe of Haw R., adj. Hambleton, Robt. Donil; Jas. Donel, Hugh Brauley: CB

Cooper, Isaac   Survey   15 July 1763
220 acres on Buckhorn Cr. of Cape Fear; Ezek.

Gaskin, Wm White: SCC. 3 copies

MtGomery, William   Survey   18 July 1763
230 acres on waters of Little River, joins Jas. Lattie, Thos. Dunagin, Wm Churton; Jas. Lattie, Nath Lewis: SCC. 3 copies.

Laughlen, Richard   Survey   18 July 1763
473 acres on Marys Cr. of Haw R.; Hugh Laughlen, Richard Laughlen: SCC. two copies

Forbus, Arthur   Survey   20 July 1763
651 acres on waters of Burch Cr. of Haw R., joins Wm Wiley, Wm Forbis; Wm Wiley, Saml Lackey: SCC. 3 copies

Graves, Thomas   Survey   20 July 1763
467 acres on waters of Rocky R., joins Peter Youngblood; Wm Grave, Wm Moffit: SCC. 3 copies.

Carr, David   Survey   20 July 1763
553 acres on S. Buffallow, joins John Danoliss (Donal) corner Arthor Forbus, Saml. Lackey: CB. 3 copies

Latta, James   Survey   23 July 1763
144 acres on waters of Enoe, joins sd Latta, Thos. Holden; Jno Latta, Robt Davis: SCC. 3 copies.

Watson, James   Survey   23 July 1763
400 acres on Elebys Cr. of Enoe; Wm Reed, Paul Harmon: SCC. 2 copies.

Sutherland, Mordecai   Survey   24 July 1763
175 acres on Cub island Cr. of Enoe, joins McCullochs line; Jno Spencer, Phillip Dosset: SCC. 3 copies.

Shepherd, Andrew   Survey   26 July 1763
552 acres on Bush Cr. of Cap Fear, joins the King's line; Thos Ballard, Jno Ballard: SCC. 3 copies

Boyd, John   Survey   27 July 1763
700 acres on Great Troublesome of Haw R., joins Peter Willson; Chris Vandegriff, Wm Dunn: SCC.

Camp, Edward   Survey   29 July 1763
245 acres on the Double Creeks of Hico, adjoins Sirratts line; Wm McCoy, Henry McCoy: SCC. 3 copies

Brooks, Robert   Survey   1 Aug 1763
178 acres on a branch of Mahoe, joins Mahoe's line; Wm Price, Wm Brooks: SCC. 3 copies

Rutherford, Patrick   Survey   8 Aug 1763
    122 acres on Lick Cr. of Flatt R.; Robt. Berry,
    Miche Robinson: SCC. 3 copies.

Justice, James   Survey   15 Aug 1763
    675 acres on Deep Cr. of Flatt R.; Thoms Striplin,
    Thomas Collins: SCC. 3 copies.

Jones, Willi   Survey   15 Aug 1763
    672 acres on north side Flatt R., joins Thos.
    Person, Jno. Brown; Thos. Person, Jno Cizart: SCC.
    "Entered by Jonas Griffin signed over" 2 copies.

Stout, Peter   Survey   26 Aug 1763
    247 acres on Reedy Br. of Cane Cr. of Haw R.,
    joins his former line; Wm Brown, Samuel Stout: SCC.
    3 copies.

Lloyd, Frederick   Survey   5 Sept 1763
    693 acres on waters of Collins Cr.; Thos. Griffin,
    Mattw Stroad: SCC. 3 copies.

Tapley, Hosea   Survey   5 Sept 1763
    180 acres on waters of Flatt R., joins his own
    line; Thos. Camp, Nathan Brisco: SCC. 3 copies.

Graves, John   Survey   10 Sept 1763
    328 acres on Benajahs Cr. of Countrey Line; Richd
    Lane, John Lay: SCC. 3 copies

Jones, Steven   Survey   15 Sept 1763
    325 acres on waters of Sandy Cr of Deep R.; Ed.
    McCain, Richd. Norton: SCC. 3 copies

McPherson, William   Survey   18 Sept 1763
    162 acres on waters of Cain Cr. of Haw R., joins
    John Piles; Charles Richeson, Jno Orman: SCC. 3
    copies.

McPherson, William   Survey   18 Sept 1763
    100 acres on waters of Cain Cr. of Haw R., joins
    Chamnes and Moon; Anthony Chamnes, Hugh Dillen:
    SCC.

Hart, Thomas   Survey   20 Sept 1763
    583 acres on waters of Haw R.; Geo. Elmore, Thos
    Barns: SCC.

Hart, Thos.   Survey   3 Oct 1763
    690 acres on waters of Haw R., adjoins Aron Pin-
    son; George Elmore, Thos Barns: SCC.

McFarlan (McFarland), John   Survey   3 Oct 1763
    150 acres on jonts Creek of Hico; Robert McFar-
    land, Daniel McFarland: SCC. 3 copies.

Rhodes, William   Survey   25 Oct 1763
    198 acres on waters of New Hope, joins Pickett;
    Jno Madden, Solomon Draper: SCC. 3 copies.

Arrington, Charles   Survey   27 Oct 1763
    213 acres on the Lick fork of Cape Fear, joins
    Mims, Lewis; John Arrington, Henry Brazel: SCC.

Boyd, William   Survey   1 Nov 1763
    431 acres on Little Troublesome of Haw R., adj.
    Jno Boyd; Geo. Rowland, Jas. Campbell: CB. 2 copies

Shepherd, Andrew   Survey   3 Nov 1763
    378 acres on waters of Cape Fear R.; Thos Ballard,
    Jno Ballard: SCC. 3 copies.

Harrison, William   Survey   10 Nov 1763
    198 acres on Little troublesome Cr. of Haw R.,
    joins Peter King; Giles Tillet, Wm Young: SCC. 3
    copies   :

Crittenden, John & Elizabeth   Assignment   10 Oct 1764
    Assign to John Alston right in lands (No descript-
    ion).
    Addressed to: Joseph Montfort
    Witnesses: John Alston, Dolling Jones.

ORANGE COUNTY RECORDS, VOL. I

GRANVILLE PROPRIETARY OFFICE PAPERS, ABSTRACTS

INDEX OF NAMES

If the name appears more than once on a page, the number of entries is in parentheses after the page number.

Abercromby, Robert 40
    Robt. 23
Acock, James 8(2), 14
Adaniel, John, Jr. 47
    William 47
    (See also: O' Daniel)
Akin, Joseph 47
Aldridge, John 22
    Joseph 35
    Nathaniel 32(2)
    Soloman 16
    Wm. 4
    (See also: Aldrige, Alldrid, & Alridge)
Aldrige, Nathaniel 32, 35(2)
    William 12
    (See also: Aldridge, Alldrid, & Alridge)
Alexander, James 11
    Thomas 47(3), 48
Alldrid, Thomas 12
    (See also: Aldridge, Aldrige, and Alridge)
Allen 16
    John 1
    Morrell 16
    Samuel, Orphan of 17
Allison 26
    James 48
    Josh 40
    (See also: Ellison)
Allred, Soloman 12
    Wm. 21
    (See also: Allrid, Alred)
Allrid, John 12
    (See also: Allred, Alred)
Alman, Ed 44
Alred, John 31
    Soloman 26, 31
    (See also: Allred, Allrid)
Alridge, Joseph 28, 35
    Nathaniel 48
    (See also: Aldridge, Al-

Alridge (Cont.)
    drige, & Allrid)
Alston 40
    John 30, 32, 40, 56(2)
Anderson, David 9
    James 9, 14, 21, 41
    Jas. 46
    Robert 14
    Thos. 46
Anglen 47
    James 43
    Jas. 47
Armfield, Jacob 9, 48
Armsby, Luke 13
Armstrong 36
    James 31
    John 15, 51, 54
    William 13, 22
Arnold 40(2)
Arrengton, Charles 54
    (See also: Arrington)
Arrington, Charles 56
    John 56
    (See also: Arrengton)
Ashmore, James 30
    Walter 54
Aven, Joseph 51
    (See also: Avin)
Avin, Joseph 53(2)
    (See also: Aven)
Aycock (See Acock)
Baker 4
    Absolem 40(2)
    Andrew 23, 34(2)
    Blake 27(2), 44
    Peter 53
Baldin, John 21
    (See also: Bauldin, Boldin)
Ballard, Jno. 55, 56
    Thos. 55, 56
Ballenger, Henry 15, 17
Banks, David 50
Bankson 46

Bankson (Cont.)
    (See also: Banksone)
Banksone, Capt. 21
    (See also: Bankson)
Barbe, John, Senr. 50
    Joseph 32, 40
    (See also: Barbee, Barbie, & Barby)
Barbee, Joseph 29, 30, 40
    (See also: Barbe, Barbie, & Barby)
Barber, William 49
Barbie, Joseph 45
    Rachel 41
    (See also: Barbe, Barbee, & Barby)
Barby, John 27, 29
    Joseph 20(2), 30(2)
    (See also: Barbe, Barbee, & Barbie)
Barclay, Wm. 4
Barker 54
    Nich. 54
    Nicholas 46
    Saml. 54
    Thomas 42
    William 15
Barnes, Brinasely 7
    Thos. 55
    William 34
    Wm. 34
    (See also: Barns)
Barnet 5, 15
    Hugh 8, 13, 19, 33, 35
    Humphrey 13
    Jesse 13
    Joseph 36
    Richard 14
    Samuel 12, 13
    Thomas 1, 40(2)
    William 13
    (See also: Barnett)
Barnett, Hugh 1, 5, 12, 20

Barnett (Cont.)
    Humphrey 44
    John 31, 41
    Jos. 47
    Joseph 28
    Thomas 44
    (See also:Barnet)
Barney, John 50
Barnhill, James 8
Barns, Brinsley 18
    Jacob 48
    James 18(2)
    Thos. 56(2)
    (See also: Barnes)
Barr, James 47
Barshear, Jesse 14
    Robt. 14
    Robt., Jr. 14
    (See also: Brashear, Bashire)
Bashire 27
    (See also: Barshear, Brashear)
Basket, William 30
Bauldin, John 18
    (See also: Boldin, Baldin)
Bauldry, William 41(2)
Baynes 43
    John 43
Beal, John 16
    (See also: Beals)
Beals, John 20
    John, Jr. 20
    (See also: Beal)
Beasley 3, 9
    Henry 1, 16
    Joshua 29
    (See also: Beesley, Beezly)
Beaverley 9
Bedford, Jas. 4
Beemer, Peter 53
Beesley, Henry 20(2)
    James 26, 29(3)
    (See also: Beasley, Beezly)
Beezly, Henry 48
    (See also: Beasley, Beesley)
Bell, Thomas 50
Bellwin, Robert 17
    (See also: Belvin)
Belvin, Robert 20, 45
    Robt. 20
    (See aalso: Bellwin)
Benbo 39
    Powel 39
Bennett 50
    Joseph 47
    (See also: Barnet, Barnett)

Benton, Lazarus 27
    Samuel 7
Berry 50(2)
    Robert 28, 53
    Robt. 56
    William 50(2)
Binum, Luke 45
    (See also: Bynam, Bynum)
Bird 10, 52
    Burgeon 22
    Burgon 35
    James 27, 29(2), 37
    John 10
    Joseph 54
    (See also: Burd)
Black, Peter 28, 34(2)
Blackley, James 45
Blackson, William 10
Blackwood 10
    William 2(2), 8
Blake, Wm. 18
Blakely, James 27, 34(2), 35, 36, 39, 45
    Jas. 45
Blalock 3(2)
    John 4
Bledsoe, Aaron 36
    Jacob 22, 32, 33, 35, 40(2), 45
    John 22, 36, 42
    Moses 36
Blosingam 49
Bogan, William 18
    (See also: Boggan)
Boggan 30
    Margaret 39
    Margt. 30
    Wm. 26
    (See also: Bogan)
Bohannon 41
    Duncan 16, 21, 23, 32, 36, 37, 45
    Duncan, Jr. 20
    John 11(2), 14(2), 16
    Joseph 20
Boid, George 48
    John 32, 54
    (See also: Boyd)
Boilston, William 49
Boldin, John 21
    (See also: Baldin, Bauldin)
Bolin 40
    (See also: Bollin, Bolling, Bowlin, Bowling)
Bollin, Alexander 35

Bollin (Cont.)
    Alexr. 22, 35
    (See also: Bolin, Bolling, Bowlin, Bowling)
Bolling, Benjamin 25
    (See also: Bolin, Bollin, Bowlin, Bowling)
Booker, John 36(2), 42
Boon, Jacob 51(2), 53
Booth, Daniel 41
    John 41, 44
Bowie, James 7, 23, 24, 35(2), 50,, 52(2)
    Jas. 24, 34
    John 48
    ----- 40
Bowlin, Benj. 6
    Benjamin 7
    (See also: Bolin, Bolliin, Bolling, Bowling)
Bowling, Benja. 36(2)
    Benjamin 47
    (See also: Bollin, Bollin, Bolling, Bowlin)
Boyd, Jno. 56
    John 2, 5(2), 6, 8, 25, 37, 45, 55
    John, Jr. 8, 14, 52
    William 54, 56
    (See also: Boid)
Bracewell, Henry 43
    Richard 35
    William 35
    (See also: Braswell)
Bracher, John 12, 21
Bradford 20
    David 29(2)
    Phileman 20, 28
    Thomas 20
Braizier, Thomas 50
Brally, Hugh 20
Brannon 47
Branson, Thomas 12
    Thos. 19
Brantley, Jno. 37
    John 25, 37
    John, Jr. 48
    Joseph 21(2), 33(2), 37
    Lewis 21, 28
Brashear, Bazel 44
    Bazil 6, 8, 10, 21(2)
    Jesse (?), 8(2), 10, 28
    Middleton 7, 8, 51
    Otho 8
    Phillip 54

Brashear (Cont.)
    Robert 8, 10, 21(2), 44
    Robert Samuel 8, 23, 28
    Robert, Senr. 28
    (See also: Barshear, Bashire, Brashears)
Brashears, Midleton 44
    (See also: Barshear, Bashire, Brasheaar)
Braswell 14
    Valentine 10
    (See also: Bracewell)
Brauley, Hugh 55
Braxon, William 21
    Wm. 21(2)
Bray, Edmd. 9
    Henry 46
    Henry, Jr. 50
Brazel, Henry 56
    Richd. 42
Bredin, Alexr. 52
    Robert 52
    (See also: Breeding)
Breeding, Robert 55
    (See also: Breedin)
Brewer, Henry 23, 25, 50
    Oliver 50
    Sackfield 17, 25
Bridges, James 39, 42, 44
    John 44
    Joseph 1
Brisco, Nathan 56
Britt, John 36
Brock, Frederick 27
Brogden 17
Brooks 41, 51, 54(2)
    Isaac 44
    Jas. 54
    Joab 39, 44, 53
    Joel 29, 30, 54
    John 11, 19
    John, Esq. 4
    Mark 44
    Robert 55
    Robert, Sr. 53
    Thomas 34
    Thos. 19
    Wm. 41, 54, 55
Brother Peter 37
Brown, Daniel 30, 31
    David 19, 23, 26, 51, 54(2)
    James 20
    Jno. 56
    John 4, 39, 40, 43, 53
    William 51

Brown (Cont.)
    Wm. 42, 56
Buckles, Abram. 28
Bucknall, Francis 10(2)
    Sarah 10
    Thomas 10
Buckner, Jno. 55
Bullock, Richard 3, 4, 32(2), 40,
    Wm. 40
    Zachariah 40
Bumpas, John 39, 40
    Robert 44
    (See also: Bumpass)
Bumpass 4
    Ed 43
    Jno. 4
    John 39, 40, 42
    Robert 43
    Samuel 4(2), 42, 43
    (See also: Bumpas)
Bunrick, Nich 37
Burd 47
    John 19(2)
    (See also: Bird)
Burgamy, William 33
Burk 48
    Richd. 42
Burney, John 53
    Willm. 20
Burt, John 18, 21, 25
Bustar, William 12
Byas, Wm. 4
Bynam, John 26
    (See also: Binum, Bynum)
Bynum, James 20(2)
    Luke 42
    (See also: Binum, Bynam)
Cabe, Barney 45
Cadles, Zachary 49
Cagle, Charles 46
Cammel, Thos. 1
Camp, Edward 52, 55
    Edwd. 43
    John 28, 36(2), 43
    Thos. 56
Campbel, John 13
    (See also: Campbell)
Campbell 48
    Duncan 8, 14
    Jas. 56
    John 30, 42
    Matthew 30
    (See also: Campbel)
Cane, Elisha 42, 53(2)
Cantrel 52

Cantrel (Cont.)
    Isaac 29
    James 31, 39
    John 26
    Joseph 26
    (See also: Cantrell, Cantril)
Cantrell, Isaac 7, 31, 39
    John 7
    (See also: Cantrel, Cantril)
Cantril, Jos. 23
    (See also: Cantrel, Cantrell)
Capper, Thomas 45
Caps. Matthew 23
Cardon, Wm. 36
Cargan, John 24
    (See also: Carragan)
Carinton, John 35
    (See also: Carrington, Carrinton)
Carmichael, Jno. 4
    John 2, 4
    Jos. 4
    Thomas 2
    Thos. 4(2)
    William 3
    Willm. 4
Carr, David 52, 55
Carragan, John 28
    (See also: Caragan)
Carrington 40
    John 40, 53
    (See also: Carinton, Carrinton)
Carrinton, John 35
    (See also: Carinton, Carrington)
Carrol, William 5
Carruther, Widow 47
    (See also: Carruthers)
Carruthers, Joseph 13
    (See also: Carruther)
Carson, Alexander 17, 20, 24
    John 23, 35
    Robt. 54
Carter, Charles 8
    Finch 15, 39
    James 17
    Nathan 51
    Timothy 43
Cary, Nathaniel 39
    Nathl. 30
Castlebury, John 41
Caswel 14
    (See also: Caswell)
Caswell, Mr. 6, 45

Caswell (Cont.)
    Richard 2, 10
    (See also: Caswel)
Cate 9, 25
    John 26, 28, 32(3), 35
    John, Junr. 25
    Joseph 14, 25, 26
    Robert 7, 11, 20, 25, 28
    Thomas 17
    Thomas, Jr. 7(2)
    Thomas, Sr. 7
    Thos. 10, 25(2)
    Thos., Jr. 14
    Thos., Senr. 26
    Thos., Sr. 14
    (See also: Cates, Kate)
Cater, James 44
Cates, Capt. 11
    Robert 29, 32, 34
    Robt. 31, 35, 39, 48
    Thomas 5
    (See also: Cate, Kate)
Chambers, Ed. 44
    Edwd. 20, 52
    William 12, 13, 38
    Wm. 12, 19
    Wm., Junr. 15
Chamnes 56
    Anthony 46, 56
Chavers 2
Cheek, James 29, 39
Cheney, James 12
Cheyney, Francis 47
Church 51
    Thomas 10, 15
    Thos. 52
Churton 14, 22, 26, 29, 31, 49
    Mr. 50
    William 1, 5(3), 7, 9, 18,
        23(2), 24(2), 29, 34,
        36(2)
    William, Esq. 5
    Willm. 6
    Wm. 14, 19, 50, 53, 55
Cizart, Jno. 56
Clanton 47
Clapp 26, 30
Clark 33
    John 31
Claton, Benone 39(2), 44
Clement, Benjamin 26
    (See also: Clements)
Clements, Benjamin 15
    (See also: Clement)
Clemons 36

Clenten, Charles 25
    (See also: Clenton, Clinten, Clinton)
Clenton, Charles 49
    Edward 49
    Robert 49
    (See also: Clenten, Clinten, Clinton)
Clinten, Robert 1
    (See also: Clenten, Clenton, Clinton)
Clinton, Robert 23
    (See also: Clenten, Clenton, Clinten)
Cole, Daniel 27
    John 51, 54
    (See also: Coole)
Colins 40
    Thomas 40
    (See also: Collings, Collins)
Collings, Thomas 33
    (See also: Colins, Collins)
Collins, Dennis 1, 5
    Hezekiah 2, 18
    James 5, 20, 21(2), 41
    Jno. 55
    John 23, 31
    Paul 44
    Paul, Mulatto 33
    Thomas 33, 44, 56
    Thos. 34
    (See also: Colins, Collings)
Colson, Ann. 35
Comb, William 3
    (See also: Combs)
Comber, J. 26
    Joseph 38
    (See also: Commer)
Combs, William 1, 9, 23, 29
    Wm 7, 9, 10, 14, 27(2), 29, 3
    (See also: Comb)
Commer, Joseph 26
    (See also: Comber)
Conner, Jno. 24(2)
    John 24, 26
Cook, Arthur 8, 14
Coole, John 51
    (See also: Cole)
Cooper, Isaac 52, 55
Copeland 7
    James 36(2), 41
    Mr. 48
    Nicholas, Junr. 49
    Richard 40, 48
    Thomas 44, 46

Copeland (Cont.)
    Thos. 45
    Wm. 41
    (See also: Copland)
Copestick, Thos. 25
Copland, James 39
    Jeames 39
    Nicholas 39(2), 39
    (See also: Copeland)
Corbel 37
Corbin, Col. 7, 18, 29
    Colo. 16
    Fra. 26
    Francis, Esq. 36
Corley, Robert 47
Couch, James 42, 45(2), 50
    Matt 50(2)
    Matthew 24
    Thos. 24, 30
    William 18, 24
Cox 17, 26, 38
    Benja. 31
    Benjamin 15, 31(2)
    Harmon 30, 31(2)
    Herman 51
    Hermon 26
    John 26, 30, 31
    Peter 38
    Saml. 26, 31
    Samuel 26, 28, 31
    Solo. 38
    Solom. 38
    Soloman 28
    Solomon 30
    Thomas 30, 31
    Thos. 13, 31(3)
    William 24, 30, 31, 37
    William, Senior 17
    Willm. 13, 29
    Wm. 30, 31, 38, 39
Craford 12
    James 29
    Jas. 29
    (See also: Crawford)
Craven, Peter 34, 39(2), 44
    Thomas 44
Crawford, James 25, 30
    (See also: Craford)
Creage, William 10
    (See also: Creague)
Creague, John 26
    (See also: Creage)
Crittenden, Elizabeth 56
    John 56
Croddin, William 16

Cromby, Robt. 23
Crow, James 44
    John 46
Culberson, Andw. 44
    Saml. 44
    (See also: Culverson)
Culbertson, James 23
Culp, Filman 28
Culverson, Samuel 39(2)
    (See also: Culberson)
Cunningham 31
    John 31
    Thomas 51
Curria, James 12
Curtis, Richard 21
Cury, Nathaniel 50
Cussick 21, 26
Daniel, John 2, 22
    (See also: Daniels)
Daniels, William 18
    (See also: Daniel)
Danielson, Robert 1
Dannall 17
    Thomas 17
Danoliss, John 55
Daves 9
Davey, Gabriel 44
    (See also: Davie, Davy)
Davidson, John 7
Davie, Gabriel 37, 42
    (See also: Davey, Davy)
Davis 26
    Adam 42, 46
    Benjamin 52, 55
    David 50
    Ellathan 46
    James 49
    Joseph 21
    Robert 22(2)
    Robt. 55
    Thomas 15
    Thos. 15
    Wm. 21
Davy 38
    Gabriel 38
    (See also: Davey, Davie)
Dawson, Wm 25
Day, Francis 27, 29, 39(2)
    Hennry 15
    John 45, 51
    Mary 17
    Mary, Jr. 25
Days 13
Dean, John 25
Deason, Benj. 5

Decern, Francis 42
Denney, Edmond 22
    (See also: Denny)
Dennis, John 6, 9, 39(2), 45
Denny 41
    Edmond 22
    James 38(3), 41
    William 25
    Zach. 54
    Zachariah 51
    (See also: Denney)
Devinport, Francis 44
Dicken, James 5
    (See also: Dickens, Dickings, Dickins)
Dickens, James 20, 32, 35(2)
    Shadrick 40
    (See also: Dicken, Dickings, Dickins)
Dickie, Mr. 11
Dickings, James 32
    (See also: Dicken, Dickens, Dickins)
Dickins, James 35
    (See also: Dicken, Dickens, Dickings)
Dickson, Henry 5, 15(2), 44
    Michael 5, 27, 38, 44
    Michl. 19
    Robert 15
    Robt 5
    Simon 6
    Simond 6
    (See also: Dixon, Dixson)
Dillen, Hugh 56
    Peter 26
Dins, Jas. 35
Dixon, Joseph 48
    Simon 46
    Soloman 48(2)
    (See also: Dickson, Dixsson)
Dixson, Henry 27
    (See also: Dickson, Dixon)
Doaks, John 49
Doane, John 46
Dobbin, Hugh 3, 5(2), 14, 15, 21, 22
    (See also: Dobbins)
Dobbins, Hugh 12, 19, 22, 31
    (Seee also: Dobbin)
Dolarhide, Ezekiel 34
    (See also: Dollarhide, Dollerhide)
Dolittle, Jas. 19
    Jos. 14

    Joseph 33, 46
    (See also: Doolittle)
Dollarhide, Aquilla 34
    (See also: Dolarhide, Dollerhide)
Dollerhide, Cornilas 21
    (See also: Dolarhide, Dollarhide)
Donal, Johnn 55
    (See also: Donald, Donel, Donil, Donnel, Donnels)
Donald, Thomas 23
    (See also: Donal, Donel, Donil, Donnel, Donnels)
Donaldson 26, 47
    (See also: Donelson)
Donel, Jas. 55
    (See also: Donal, Donald, Donil, Donnel, Donnels)
Donelson 27
    (See also: Donaldson)
Donil, Robt. 55
    (See also: Donal, Donald, Donel, Donnel, Donnels)
Donnel 20
    (See also: Donal, Donald, Donel, Donil, Donnels)
Donnels 28
    (See also: Donal, Donald, Donel, Donil, Donnel)
Doolittle, Joseph 47
    (See also: Dolittle)
Dosset, Phillip 55
Dover 24
    John 21
Dowdy 49
Dowell, John 1
Downs, Zachy 6(2)
Dowther, Geo. 14
Draper, Soloman 56
Duckworth 46
Dunagan, John 26, 30, 36
    Thomas, Junr. 50
    Thos. 36
    (See also: Dunagin, Dunnagan, Dunnagin)
Dunagin 34
    John 34(2), 40
    Thos. 34, 55
    (See also: Dunagan, Dunnagan, Dunnagin)
Dunkin, Joseph 9
Dunn, Martin 25, 36
    William 25
    Wm. 55

Dunnagan, John 18, 33
    (See also: Dunagan, Dunagin, Dunnagin)
Dunnagin, Jno. 55
    (See also: Dunagan, Dunagin, Dunnagan)
Durham, Thomas 38, 43
    Thos. 9
Dutch George 39(2)
Eason, Joshua 21, 47
Edson, Chris. 15
Edward, John 43
    (See also: Edwards)
Edwards, John 25, 38
    Thomas 32
    (See also: Edward)
Ellidge, Isaac 38
Elliman, Enos 40, 55
    Jno. 54
    John 40, 51, 55
    (See also: Ellimon)
Ellimon, Enos 55
    John 55
    (See also: Elliman)
Ellis, Benjn. 47
Ellison, John 10
    Joseph 3, 18, 36
    (See also: Allison)
Elmore, Geo. 55, 56
    George 56
Embree, John 36, 40
Emmerson, Jas. 53
Emory, John 16
Emry, Moses 9
Erwin, Robert 17, 24, 31
Evans, Jacob 7, 19
Ewing, James 50
Fairgison, John 15
    (See also: Ferguson, Farguson)
Falconer 36
    Jno 15
    John 19, 20, 26
    (See also: Faulconer)
Fanning, John 38
Farguson, John 21
    (See also: Fairguson, Ferguson)
Farmer, Samuel 35
    (See also: Ffarmer)
Faulconer, John 45
    (See also: Falconer)
Ferguson 22
    Jno. 22
    John 22

Ferguson (Cont.)
    (See also: Fairguson, Farguson)
Fershere, Charles 7
    (See also: Fooshe, Foushe, Foushee)
Few, William 33, 37, 39
Ffarmer, Saml. 28
    (See also: Farmer)
Field, Jane 25
    Robert 25
    (See also: Fields)
Fields, Jane 17
    John 41
    (See also: Field)
Fikes, Malachy 37, 38, 42
Fillot, Gile 8
    (See also: Tillet, Tillot)
Fincher 39
Findley, Andrew 54
Fisher 16(2)
Flaxon, Thos. 14, 19
    (See also: Laxon)
Flay, Jacob 43
Flinn, Geo. 38
    Thomas 44
Fooshe, Charles 18
    (See also: Fershere, Foushe, Foushee)
Forbis, Wm. 55
    (See also: Forbus)
Forbus, Arthur 52, 55
    (See also: Forbis)
Ford, Henry 1
Fornus, Arthor 55
Forrester, Jas. 10
Forster, Hugh 9
Foushe, Joseph 25
    (See also: Fershere, Fooshe, Foushee)
Foushee, Charles 7, 18, 43
    Widow 43
    (See also: Fershere, Fooshe, Foushe)
Fowler, Eliah 2
Foyel, Ratlif 30
Frazier, John 24, 31
Freeman, Gab: 13
    Gabriel 9, 26, 49
    William 41
Fulkerson, James 47
Fuller, James 23
    John 45
    Jos. 36
    Joseph 23, 28, 45

Fulsum 48
Fulton, Samuel 32(2), 34(2)
Gaddis 47
    Isaac 43
Gardner, John 37
    John, Capt. 41
Gaskin, Ezek. 55
George, David, Jr. 48
Gibson 4, 49
    Charles 35, 43
    George 33, 34, 44
    Mr. 25
    Thomas 33, 35, 43, 52
    Thos. 34, 35, 55
    Wm. 7
    (See also: Gilson)
Giles 47
    John 47
Gilson, Thomas 43
    (See also: Gibson)
Ginn, Moses 28
Gist, Nathaniel 2, 3, 4
Godwin, Barnebe 21
Goff, Henry 3
Goforth, Miles 28, 34
Gold, Joseph 41
Goodbread, Philip 48
Goodson, Wm. 20
Gordon, John 37, 38
Gorss, William 33
Gose 5
Goss 41
    William 38(2)
Gould, Ephriam 18
Governor 2, 3(2), 5, 6, 23
Gowing 27
    Alexr. 22, 27
Granville 52
    Earl 13, 39, 45
    Lord 23, 36, 422
Grave, John 54
    Wm. 55
    (See also: Graves)
Graves, John 56
    James 46
    Robt. 40
    Thomas 21, 29, 35, 46, 53, 55
    William 30, 38
    (See also: Grave)
Gray 3
    John 3(2), 11, 23, 36
Green, Thomas 18
Gregg, Jacob 51, 54
Griffen 53
    Jonas 53, 55

William 53
(See also: Griffin)
Griffin, Ralph 12
 Wm. 41
 (See also: Griffen)
Grimes, Thomas 6
Griinels, Jonathon 28
Guston, John 19
Guthrie, Wm. 13
Gwain, Robert 26
Hackoney, Lamuell 21(2)
Hadley, Jerimiah 50
Hague, John 35
Haley, David 35, 40(2), 46
Hall, James 1, 7
 John 44
Hallum, John 21
Haltam, Wm. 3
 (See also: Holton)
Ham 49
 Widow 43
Hambellon, George 52
 (See also: Hambelton, Hamelton, Hamilton)
Hambelton 55
 (See also: Hambellon, Hamelton, Hamilton)
Hamelton, Ninean Bell 48
 (See also: Hambellon, Hambelton, Hamilton)
Hamilton, Thomas 17, 20
 Thos. 20
 (See also: Hambellon, Hambelton, Hamelton)
Hammond, John 2
Hampton, James 3
 Jas. 4
Hanna, Jno. 15
Hardee, John 41
Harden 55
 Benjamin 47
 Jonathon 522
Harding, Eliz. 11
Hargrove, Richard 4, 26
Harlan, Aaron 10, 18
Harmon, John 11
 Paul 55
Harper, Mr. 3
 Robert 1
Harratt, James 38
Harrel, Burges 38
Harrelson, Burges 52, 55
 Burgess 52
 Elisha 55
 Paul 55 (2)

Harrelson (Cont.)
 (See also: Harrilson)
Harrilson, Paul 44
 (See also: Harrelson)
Harris, Thompson 15, 46, 47
 Thomson 13, 14(5), 19
Harrison, Thomas 45
 William 54, 56
Harrot, James 37
Hart, David 13, 19(2), 22, 35
 James 6
 Nathaniel 48
 Nathl. 35
 Thomas 47, 49, 52, 53, 54, 55, 56
 Thos. 49, 56
Hartso, Philip 38, 44
Harvey, John 18
 Michael 46
 William 42, 46
Hasting, Henry 3, 37
Hatley, John 8, 15, 19, 20(2)
 Sherrod 20(2)
Hawkins, James 52
Hays, Patrick 2
Haywood, Col. Jno. 6
 Jno. 21
 Sherwood 15, 227
Head, Stophel 21
Hearn, George 20
Helmes, Wm. 9
Hembre, David 28, 35
Hembree 28
Henderson, Argalus 30, 45
 Hercules 23
 Richd. 12
Herinnlon, George 44
 (See also: Herndon, Herrendon)
Herndon, Geo. 35, 37
 George 24, 37
 (See also: Herinnlon, Herrendon)
Herrendon, George 50
 (See also: Herinnlon, Herndon)
Herring, Mr. 45
Hide, Benjamin 27
Higdon, John, Jr. 34
Hightower, Austin 6, 9, 45
Hill, Charles 2
 Nicholas 22
 Nickalis 19
 Nikolas 22
 Thomas 19, 21

Him, George 28
Hinche, John 42
 (See also: Hinchie, Hinchy)
Hinchie, John 38
 (See also: Hinche, Hinchy)
Hinchy, John 37
 (See also: Hinche, Hinchie)
Hines, Robt. 14
Hinton, William 39(2), 42, 45
Hobson, George 9, 18
 George, Jr. 18(2), 31, 37, 49
 George, Sr. 31, 37
 Richard 20
 Stephen 37
Hodgens, Phillip 29
Hodges 35
 Robert 44
Hogg, Gideon 42, 46
Hoggan, Charles 3
Hogwood, James 43
Holada, Henry 55(2)
 (See also: Holeday, Holliday)
Holden, Thomas 11
 Thos. 55
Holdman, Richard 28
 (See also: Holeman, Holman, Holoman)
Holeday, Henry 52
 (See also: Holada, Holliday)
Holeman 34
 Richard 20, 34
 Richd. 35(2), 39
 (See also: Holdman, Holeman, Holman, Holoman)
Holensworth 55
 (See also: Holingsworth, Hollingsworth, Hollinsworth)
Holifield, Wm. 30, 33
 (See also: Holyfield)
Holingsworth, Jesse 49
 (See also: Holensworth, Hollingsworth, Hollinsworth)
Hollan, James 54
Holles, Moses 22, 27
Holliday, Henry 12, 21(2)
 (See also: Holada, Holeday)
Hollingsworth 11
 Jesse 19
 Valentine 12, 19
 (See also: Holensworth, Holingsworth, Hollinsworth)
Hollinsworth 18
 Valentine 11
 (See also: Holensworth, Holingsworth, Hollingsworth)

Holman, Richard 10
    (See also: Holdman, Holeman, Holoman)
Holoman, Richard 20(2)
    (See also: Holdman, Holeman, Holman)
Holsenbeck, Derrick 51
    (See also: Holsenpack)
Holsenpack, Derick 54
    (See also: Holsenbeck)
Holt, Jacob 27
    Michal 26, 27
    Michl. 25
Holtom, William 3(2)
    (See also: Haltam)
Holyfield, Ralph 40(2), 41
    William 32(40
    Wm. 41
    (See also: Holifield)
Hooker, William 48
Hooper 48
Hopkins, John 15, 21
    Lambeth 21
    Wm. 4
Hopper, Wm. 4
Hopson, Edward 25
Horton, James 4(2), 6(2), 29, 40, 49
    William 34
Howard, Phillip 6
    Stephen 13, 19(3)
Howe, Charles 54
Howell, Lewis 21
Howlet, William 9
    (See also: Howlett)
Howlett 21
    William 18(2)
    (See also: Howlet)
Hues, John 27
    (See also: Huges, Hughes, Hughs)
Huges, John 21
    (See also: Hues, Hughes, Hughs)
Hughes, Charles 48
    John 12
    Thomas 22(2)
    (See also: Hues, Huges, Hughs)
Hughs 13
    John 12
    Saml. 13
    Thomas 35
    (See also: Hues, Huges, Hughes)
Humphrays, William 33

Humphrays (Cont.)
    (See also: Humphrey, Humphreys, Humphries, Humphys, Umphries)
Humphrey, Griffin 28
    Wm. 36
    (See also: Humphrays, Humphreys, Humphries, Humphys Umphries)
Humphreys, Griffen 32
    Wm. 35
    (See also: Humphrays, Humphrey, Humphries, Humphy, Umphries)
Humphries 41
    William 33
    (See also: Humphrays, Humphrey, Humpohreys, Humphys, Umphries)
Humphys, Wm. 33
    (See also: Humphrays, Humphrey, Humphreys, Humphries, Umphries)
Hunley, Darbey 41
Hunt, Eleazer 30, 31
Hunter, Elisha 48
    Jno. 27
    John 24, 25, 27, 37
    Sam 3
Hurley, John 41, 47
Husband 25
    Harman 1
    Herman 1, 8(2), 9, 12(2), 13(2), 16, 19, 22, 25(2), 28, 31(2), 35, 41, 43, 48, 49(2), 52, 54
Hussey, Christopher 44
Innes 16
Isom, Ed 35
Jackson 28
    Isaac 2, 6, 8, 9(2), 17, 20, 24, 45(2)
    Thos. 9
    W. 45
    William 9, 26
    Wm. 24
Jacob, Shadrack 38
James, Thomas 19, 20
Jarret 50
Jay, William 22, 33(2)
Jefferies, Osborn 17
    (See also: Jeffrey, Jeffreys, Jeffries, Jeffreys)
Jeffrey, Capt. 20
    (See also: Jeffries, Jeffreys,

Jeffrey (Cont.)
    Jeffries, Jeffreys)
Jeffreys 33(2)
    Osborn 3(2), 27, 33(2), 34
    Osborne 34
    Osburn 4, 21
    (See also: Jefferies, Jeffrey, Jeffries, Jeffrys)
Jeffries, Osborn 34, 39, 41
    (See also: Jefferies, Jeffrey, Jeffreys, Jeffrys)
Jeffrys, Osborn 45
    (See also: Jefferies, Jeffrey, Jeffreys, Jeffries)
Jenkins, David 44
    Samuel 32
    (See also: Jinkins)
Jinkins, Samuel 41
    (See also: Jenkins)
Johqson, Aaron 36
Johnston 50
    Gov. 14, 16, 24
    Henry 2
    John 8
    William 10
Jones, Charles 29, 39
    Dolling 56
    Edward, Capt. 21
    Francis 11(2), 19, 27(2), 28, 30, 45, 52, 55
    Henry 49
    Jacob 43
    John 6, 11, 29
    Nathaniel 45
    Robert 36, 42, 51
    Robt. 36, 50
    Stephen 53
    Steven 56
    Tignal 1
    Vincent 41
    Willi. 56
    Wm. 53
Joyce, Michael 15
Julian, George 31
    Isaac 49
    John 49
Justice, James 53, 56
Kaddle, Zachary 30
Kain, Daniel 14
Kate, John 5
Keesy, Woolrick 45
Kell, Thomas 51
    Thos. 54
Kelly, John 14
Kenady 5

Kenady, Cont.)
    Andrew 36
    (See also: Kennedy, Kenniday, Kennidy)
Kendrick, James 49
Kennedy, William 7
    Wm 26
    (See also: Kenady, Kenniday, Kennidy)
Kenniday 55
    (See also: Kenady, Kennedy, Kennidy)
Kennidy, Wm. 14
    (See also: Kenady, Kennedy, Kenniday)
Kerby, Jas. 15
    John 15
    William 36
    (See also: Kirby)
Kerksey, Christopher 29, 31
    Jas. 31
    (See also: Kirksey)
Key, Henry 25, 29, 36
Kilgore, Robert 13, 15, 22
Kimbrough 36
    Duke 8(2)
    Marmaduke 2, 6
    Nathaniel 7, 23, 25, 30, 32(2), 33
    Nathl. 36
Kincheloe, John 26
King 55
    Benajah 14
    John 27(2), 43, 45, 47, 50, 54
    Johnston 47
    Joseph 34
    Peter 2, 5, 14, 35(3), 40, 56
    Thomas 50
Kirby, James 15
    William 36
    (See also: Kerby)
Kirk 33
    Geo. 37
    Joseph 33, 37
Kirks, Joseph 37
Kirksey, Edward 38, 43
    (See also: Kerksey)
Knowls, Benja 14(3)
Konody, Vendorgrove 53
    (See also: Thonody)
Lacey, William 46
    (See also: Lasey)
Lackey, Saml. 55(2)
    (See also: Lackkie)
Lackkie, Allexander 9

Lackkie (Cont.)
    (See also: Lackey)
Lackston 22
Lambert 21
Lan__, John 6
Landers, Thos. 23
Landrum, Benjamin 40(2), 45
    Benjn. 45
    Jno. 8
    John 7, 37(3), 40(2), 45
    John, Jr. 40, 41
    John, Sr. 40(2)
Lane, Jesse 15(2)
    Joseph 13, 15(2)
    Joseph, Jr.
    Richard 46
    Richd. 56
    Wm. 13
Lankson, Absolom 44
Lantrop, Thomas 44, 45
Lantrum, Thomas 14
Lapsley, Thomas 37
    (See also: Lapslie)
Lapslie, Thomas 30
    (See also: Lapsley)
Lasey, Wm. 46
    (See also: Lacey)
Lathem, James 48
    (See also: Letham)
Latta 55
    James 53, 55
    Jno. 55
    (See also: Lattie)
Lattie, Jas. 55(2)
    (See also: Latta)
Laughlan 54
    Hugh 11, 18(2)
    Richard 52
    (See also: Laughlen, Laughlin, Laughlone)
Laughlen, Hugh 55
    Richard 55(2)
    (See also: Laughlan, Laughlin, Laughlone)
Laughlin, Hugh 28
    (See also: Laughlan, Laughlen, Laughlone)
Laughlone 51
    (See also: Laughlan, Laughlen, Laughlin)
Lawford, James 14
Lawrence, James 42
    Jno. 41
    John 19, 37
Laxon, Thomas 15

Laxon (Cont.)
    Thos. 19
    (See also: Flaxon, Laxson, Laxton)
Laxson, Thomas 33
    Thos. 44
    (See also: Flaxon, Laxon, Laxton)
Laxton 40(2)
    Thomas 12, 46
    Thos. 27
    (See also: Flaxon, Laxon, Laxson)
Lay, John 33, 56
Lea, George 21
    James 2
    John 35(2), 39, 41, 45, 47, 48, 49, 50(2)
    Major 46
    Mr. 50
    Zachariah 50
    (See also: Lee)
Leavens, Nicholas Perkins 50
Leavin, Jacob 42(2)
Lee, William 18, 21
    John 5
    (See also: Lea)
Leftear, Leonard 25
Lehugh, Peter 20
Lemmon, Henry 33
Lemmone, Henry 37
Leper, Jeremiah 46
Letham, James 42
    (See also: Latham)
Lewis 13, 26, 56
    Enoch 1, 3, 11, 12, 19, 42(2)
    Nath. 55
Lincecum, Gideon 47
    (See also: Linchicome, Linchicum, Lincicum)
Linch, John 49
    (See also: Linche)
Linche, Edward 37
    (See also: Linch)
Linchicome, Gedion 24
    Gideon 24
    (See also: Lincecum, Linchicum, Lincicum)
Linchicum, Giden 39
    Gideon 41
    (See also: Lincecum, Linchicome, Lincicum)
Lincicum, Giden 47
    (See also: Lincecum, Linchicome, Linchicum)

Lindley 26
    James 18, 21(4)
    Simon 21
    Thomas 16, 19, 52
    Thos. 18, 52
    William 52
    (See also: Lindly, Linly)
Lindly, James 51
    (See also: Lindley, Linly)
Linen, Hugh 52(2)
Linley, James 54
    Thomas, Senr. 11
    Thos. 11
    (See also: Lindley, Lindly)
Linval, Thomas, Jr. 3, 6
    (See also: Linvall)
Linvall, Thomas, Jr. 4
    Thomas, Sr. 4
    Thos., Sr. 4
    Wm 4(2)
    (See also: Linval)
Lively, Bethel 14
Lloyd 17
    Capt. 27
    Frederick 53, 56
    Thomas 15
    Thomas, Esq. 47
    Thos. 6
    (See also: Loyd)
Logue, John 14
Long, Benja 27(2)
    Benjamin 22
    James 27(3)
    John 41
    Mary 51
    William 7, 11
Lott, William 51
Lovelatty, Marshal 14
Lowe 48
    Robt. 8
    Thomas 43
    Thos. 44
Loyd 6
    Thos., Jr. 6
    (See also: Lloyd)
Lucus, Wm 4
Lune 38
Mabry, Francis 17
Macfarland, Robt. 35(2)
    (See also: McFarlan, McFarland, McFarlin)
Mackie, Watson & Co. 48
Mackin, Alexander 25
Madden, Jno. 56
    (See also: Maden)

Maddock 24
    Joseph 31(2), 35
Maden 37
    John 38
    (See also: Madden)
Mafitt, William 30, 31
    (See also: Moffit, Moffitt)
Maho 53
    (See also: Mahoe, Mayho, Mayo, Mayor)
Mahoe 55
    (See also: Maho, Mayho, Mayo, Maayor)
Mangum, Arthur 52, 55
Manning, William 52
Marler, David 50
Marr, Christopher 35
Marsh 54
    John 18, 23, 25(2)
    Robert 18
    Robt. 24, 45, 54
    William 9, 18, 51
    William, Jr. 18
    Wm 9, 24, 25(22)
Marten, William 37
    Zachariah 37
    (See also: Martin)
Martin 54
    George 2, 18, 35
    John 7(2), 8, 18(2), 33
    John, Esq. 18
    Peter 16, 20
    William 2, 11, 18
    Zach. 5, 11, 12
    Zach., Senr. 11
    Zachariah 2(2), 7, 8, 18, 19, 30, 43, 44, 51, 53
    Zachariah, Capt. 46, 48
    Zachariah, Jr. 31, 38, 46
    Zachariah, Senr. 12, 16
    Zack. 9
    Zack., Sr. 8
    (See also: Marten)
Massey, Richd 33, 41(2)
Mateer, Robert 31
    Robt. 31(2)
    William 31(2), 53, 55(2)
    Wm. 55
    (See also: Mateere, Mecteere)
Mateere, Robert 31
    (See also: Mateer, Mecteere)
Matthews, George 51, 54
    Walter 21
Mattock, Joseph 11, 16
Mauldin, Benja 36

    Richard 25(2)
    Richd. 36
Maxwell, John 12
May, John 48
Mayho 22, 33, 35, 45
    Jas. 22
    (See also: Maho, Mahoe, Mayo, Mayor)
Mayo 15, 35, 40
    (See also: Maho, Mahoe, Mayho, Mayor)
Mayor 27
    (See also: Maho, Mahoe, Mayho, Mayo)
McCain, Ed 54, 56
McCallaster, James 7
    (See also: McCallester, McCallister, McClester, McLester)
McCallester, James 6
    (See also: McCallaster, McCallister, McClester, McLester)
McCallister 20
    (See also: McCallaster, McCallester, McClester, McLester)
McCarver 7, 17
    James 26
McClester, Jas. 54
    (See also: McCallaster, McCallester, McCallister, McLester)
McCormick 29
    John 29
McCoy, Henry 55
    Wm. 55
McCrackon, Alexander 28, 29
    (See also: McCrakon)
McCrakon 25
    (See also: McCrackon)
McCullem, Henry 10
    (See also: McCullom)
McCulloch 22, 32, 40(2), 42, 46, 51, 53, 55
    (See also: McCullock, McCullogh, McCulloh, McCulough)
McCullock 7, 27, 32
    (See also: McCulloch, McCullough, McCulloh, McCullough)
McCullogh 1
    Capt. 4
    (See also: McCulloch, McCullock, McCulloh, McCullough)
McCulloh 3, 30
    (See also: McCulloch, McCullock, McCullogh, McCullough)
McCullom, John 14(3)
    (See also: McCullem)

McCullough, Mr. 40
    (See also: McCulloch, McCullock, McCullogh, McCulloh)
McDaniel, Alexander 26
    John 12, 20, 22, 52
    (See also: McDaniell, McDaniels)
McDaniell 22
    (See also: McDaniel, McDaniels)
McDaniels, John 49
    (See also: McDaniel, McDaniell)
McDanold, James 33
    (See also: McDonnel)
McDeade, Cornelius 20
McDonnel, John 26
    (See also: McDanold)
McFarlan, John 54, 56
    (See also: Macfarland, McFarland, Mcfarlin)
McFarland, Big Robert 47
    Daniel 56
    John 56
    Robert 56
    (See also: Macfarland, McFarlan, Mcfarlin)
McFarlin 12, 33(2)
    (See also: Macfarland, McFarlan, McFarland)
McFastern, Willm 6
McFerson, Wm 31
    (See also: McPherson)
McGee 17, 54
    John 49
    John, Capt. 43
    John, Esq. 43
McGowan, James, Jr. 51
    (See also: McGowen, McGowin)
McGowen, James, Jr. 46
    Peter 38
    (See also: McGowan, McGowin)
McGowin, James, Jr. 24
    John 21(3), 26, 34
    (See also: McGowan, McGowen)
McKee, Anne 26
    (See also: McKey)
McKey, Anne 18
    (See also: McKee)
McKinsey, Andrew 9
McLester, Joseph 27, 30(2)
    (See also: McCallaster, McCallaster, McCallister, McClester)
McManamy, John 31
McMillan 14, 19
McNeil, Hector 43
McNight 36

McNight (Cont.)
    John 17, 28
    (See also: Night)
McParson 38
McPerson, William 26
McPherson, William 53(2), 56(2)
    (See also: Mcferson)
McVay, Daniel 50
    (See also: McVey)
McVey 50(2)
    Daniel 50, 52(22)
    (See also: McVay)
McWhorter, George 40(2), 41
Mears, William 16
Meban 25, 26
    William 17
    (See also: Mebane)
Mebane 54
    Alexander 16
    Willm. 51
    (See also: Meban)
Mecteere, James 38
    Robert 38
    William 37
    (See also: Mateer, Mateere)
Melborn, William, Junr. 43
Melton, Nathan 23, 31(2), 39(2), 44
Merit, Stephen 52
Merrett, Anne 1
Michal, John 54
Miers, David 6
    Wm 6
Miles, Abram 40
    Jno. 43, 53
Miller 22
    George 18, 21
Mills, John 20
    William 2, 8
    Wm, Jr. 8
Milton, Isom 36
    Robert 22
Mim, Drury 54
Mims 56
Minnis 46
Mitchel 11, 46
    Robert 51, 54
    (See also: Mitchell)
Mitchell 16
    Andrew 23, 24
    Andrew, Esq. 16, 26
    Andw. 11
    David 23, 31, 51
    Esq. 9
    Robt. 13
    (See also: Mitchel)

Moffit, Wm. 55
    (See also: Maffitt, Moffitt)
Moffitt, Hugh 42
    (See also: Maffitt, Moffit)
Mole, Jona 5
Montfort, Joseph 56
Montgomery, William 53
    (See also: MtGomery)
Moon 56
    James 53
Moony, Saml. 24
Moor, David 43
    Wm. 2
    (See also: Moore)
Moore 18
    Charles 20(2)
    David 47
    (See also: Moor
Mordack, James 26(2)
Mora, Edward 34
    (See also: Taylor)
Moreland 4
Morgan 27
    Capt. 32
    Joshua 18
    Mark 6, 9(2), 20, 22(3), 23, 42, 49(2), 50(3)
    Mark, Capt. 26, 27, 29(3)
    Thomas 52
Morley, Jacob 9
Mororaty, Robert 28
Morris, George 31
    Henry 15, 27
    Henry, Jr. 5
Morrow, Benj. 34, 36
    Benjamin 45
    William 16
    (See also: Murray, Murrey, Murey)
Moseley, Mr. 13(2)
Moss 8
    James 8, 24
Mote, Jona 5
Motte, Jonathon 7
MtGomery, William 55
    (See also: Montgomery)
Mulkey 23, 27
Mullen 3, 7
    John 43
    Thomas 43
    William 3
Mullis 50(2)
Mumford, Joseph 39
Munchy, Phileman 17
Mundy, Arthur 31

Murdah, James 4
    Jno. 4
Murdoc, Jno. 54
    (See also: Murdock)
Murdock, John 25
    (See also: Murdoc)
Murey, John 22
    (See also: Morrow, Murray, Murrey)
Murfey, Wm 21
Murray 47
    Benja 10
    Benjamin 45
    Thomas 47
    (See also: Morrow, Murey, Murrey)
Murrey, Benja 22
    (See also: Morrow, Murey, Murray)
Nation, Capt. 25
    Christopher 25
Natt, Frederick 7
Nave, Conrad 51
Neal, Garrit 27
Needham, Jno. 41
Nelson, Abraham 20, 33, 36
    Abram 11, 20
    Alexander 26
    David 11
    George 26
    Moses 46
    Reson 31, 39
    Samle. 6
    Thomas 3, 32, 36(2), 42
    Thos. 8(2), 24
    William 30
Nethery, John 18
Newton, John 27
Nichols, Jas. 55
Nicholson, James 48
Nicks, Morgan 10
    John 17
Night 17
    (See also: McNight)
Nincho, John 36
Nipper 48
Nobles, Thomas 26
Noll 18
Norris 11
    Danl. 11
North, Thomas 25, 48
Norton, Edward 54
    Richd. 54, 56
    Stephen 26, 27, 47
Nunn 27

Nunn (Cont.)
    William 42
O'Daniel, John, Jr. 47
    (See also: Adaniel)
Oaks, John 46
Oden, Thos. 24, 27
Ogles, Harculus 47
    Hercules 49
Oldham, James 52, 54
    Jesse 54
Orman, Jno. 56
    John 52
Ormsby (See Armsby)
Owen, Richd. 11
Owens, Wm 2
Pain 52
Paine, James, Col. 27
    James, Doctor 44
Pamplen, Robert 18
Parker 14, 32(2)
    Joseph 29
    Richard 4, 8, 14
    Richard, Esq. 37(2), 41, 50
    Richd 10, 14
    Samuell 48
Parkings, Thomas 20
Parson 6
    Richd 40
    Thomas 49
    (See also: Parsons, Person)
Parsons, Richd. 35(2), 40
    (Seee also: Parson, Person)
Paterson, Gilbert 19
    (See also: Patterson)
Patterson 29, 30, 40
    Gilbert 5, 43
    H. 14
    James 43
    John 19, 41
    John, Esq. 10(2)
    Justice 10
    Robert 8, 9, 14(2), 18, 31, 38(3), 43
    (See also: Paterson)
Paulson, Paul 46
Pendergrass, Robert 43
Perkins, Peter 51
Person, Thomas 34
    Thos. 56(2)
    (See also: Parson, Parsons)
Peter 39
    (See also: Peters)
Peters 39
    (See also: Peter)
Petty, William 48, 49

Petty (Cont.)
    Willm. 29
Pettypool, Seth 35
Philip 46
    (See also: Philips, Phillips)
Philips 25
    David 31
    William 31
    (See also: Philip, Phillips)
Phillips 26
    Benjamin 31
    David 26
    David, Jr. 47
    David, Senr. 47
    Jesse 47
    John 26, 51, 52
    William 31, 42, 51
    (See also: Philip, Philips)
Picket, Micajah 25
    , Wm. 36
    (See also: Pickett)
Pickett 56
    William 10, 114(2), 54
    (See also: Picket)
Pile, John 16, 52
    (See also: Piles)
Piles, Jno. 53
    John 56
    (See also: Pile)
Pinson, Aaron 54
    Aron, 6, 56
    Joseph 2, 15
Pitman 2(2)
    Jno. 2
    (See also: Pittman)
Pittman, Saml. 39
    Wm. 39
    (See also: Pitman)
Pitts, John 46
Poe, Simon, Jr. 31, 45
    Stephen 27, 30, 31, 43, 45
Pollock 25, 28
    Cullen 25, 36
Poplin, George 37(2), 43, 53
Porter, Hugh 54
Posey, Nehemiah 45(2)
Potter, Ephriam 6
    Wm. 37
Powel 2
    Nathanl. 19
    (See also: Powell)
Powell, John 27
    Lucas 17
    Nathaniel 13, 19, 48
    Nathl. 36

Powell (Cont.)
   (See also: Powel)
Presnall, Jacob 47
Prestwood 7
Price, John 9, 38, 43
   Wm. 54, 55
Pryor 28
   John 12, 22
   John, Esq. 47
   Phillip 1, 34(3), 35
Purdum, John 38(2), 41
Pyson, Jno. 10(2)
Ragsdale 53
Rainey, Jno. 54
   John 35, 40
   William 25, 26
Rambo, Lawrence 22
Ramsey, John 41, 45
   Wm. 45(2)
Ratlif, Joel 49
Rawls, Dempsey 42
Ray, James 48
Redman, Lawrence 10(2)
Reed 27, 37, 42
   Jno. 5, 6
   Nathaniel 9
   Nathl. 13
   Rob 36
   Robert 10, 31
   Will 7
   Will, Junr. 36
   William 16, 23, 38, 52, 54
   William, Esq. 1, 21, 27, 29, 49
   Wm., Esq. 36
   Wm. 19(2), 55
   Wm. Jr. 1
Reedman, John 35
Reeves, William, Jr. 42
   Wm. 20
   Wm., Jr. 40
Rennals, James 25
   Sherrod 33, 36
   (See also: Rennols, Reynold, Reynolds, Ronnels, Ronols, Runalds, Runnal, Runnels)
Rennols, John 26
   (See also: Rennals, Reynold, Reynolds, Ronnels, Ronols, Runalds, Runnal, Runnels)
Resane, Thos. 36
Reynold, Jereh. 13
   Wm 13
   (See also: Rennals, Rennols, Reynolds, Ronnels, Ronols, Runalds,

Reynold (Cont.)
   Runnal, Runnels)
Reynolds, David 9, 13
   William 8
   (See also: Rennals, Rennols, Reynold, Ronnels, Ronols, Runalds, Runnal, Runnels)
Rhoades 14
   Christopher 14, 20(2)
   Hezekiah 17
   William 14
   Wm. 41
   (See also: Rhodes)
Rhodes, Christopher 9, 14, 18
   Hezekiah 20
   Issachar 20
   Jackson 49
   John 3, 10, 11, 49
   William 4, 10, 54, 56
   Wm. 14
   (See also: Rhoades)
Rice, William 4
   Wm 2
Richarson, Joseph 55
   (See also: Richason, Richeson)
Richason, Joseph 54
   (See also: Richarson, Richeson)
Richeson, Charles 56
   (See also: Richarson, Richason)
Rickets, Reason 34(2), 41
Ridle 40
   (See also: Riddle)
Riddle, Moses 43
   (See also: Ridle)
Rigby, John 50
   (See also: Rigsby)
Rigsby, James 27, 49
   John 49
   (See also: Rigby)
Riley, Jacob 37(2)
Roberson, John 22
   Luke 22
   (See also: Robertsonn, Robeeson, Robinson, Robison)
Roberts, Richard 34, 41
   Willis 41
   Wm. 30, 34, 35, 37(2)
Robertson, John 51
   (See also: Roberson, Robeson, Robinson, Robison)
Robeson, John 24
   (See also: Roberson, Robertson, Robinson, Robison)
Robinson, Enoch 27
   John 8, 14, 19(2), 26, 54

Robinson (Cont.)
   Miche 56
   Thomas 35, 48
   William 19
   (See also: Roberson, Robertson, Robeson, Robison)
Robison, Thomas 32
   (See also: Roberson, Robertson, Robeson, Robinson)
Roe, Cornelius 48
Ronnels, Hambleton 36
   (See also: Rennals, Rennols, Reynold, Reynolds, Ronols, Runalds, Runnal, Runnels)
Ronols, Hambleton 39
   (See also: Rennals, Rennols, Reynold, Reynolds, Ronnels, Runalds, Runnal, Runnels)
Roper, David 22
Rowland, geo. 56
Ruminger, George 24
Runalds, Dudley 22
   (See also: Rennals, Rennols, Reynold, Reynolds, Ronnels, Ronols, Runnal, Runnels)
Runnal 40
   (See also: Rennals, Rennols, Reynold, Reynolds, Ronnels, Ronols, Runnalds, Runnels)
Runnels, Jno. 4
   (See also: Rennals, Rennols, Reynold, Reynolds, Ronnels, Ronols, Runalds, Runnaal)
Russel, Arnold 40
Rutherford 28, 54
   Coll. 9
   Mr. 7
   Patrick 4, 51, 53, 55, 56
Rutledge, Jno 4
   Reason 2, 4
Salinger, Peter 41
Salling, Geo. Adam 46
Sample,, James 48
Sanfield, Robt. 35
Sargent, Steven 41
   William 41
   (See also: Sarjeant, Sarjent, Sergant)
Sarjeant, William 36(2)
   (See also: Sargent, Sarjent, Sergant)
Sarjent, William 36
   (See also: Sargent, Sarjaent, Sergant)
Sarratt 53

Satterfield, Bedwel 41
    Bedwell 43
    James 22, 42
    John 34(2)
Saxon 14, 37(4)
    Benj. 37(2)
    Benjamin 33(2), 35, 37
    Benjamn. 16
    Charles 37(3)
    Saml. 37
Scaife, William 19
    Wm. 9
Scarlet, John 41
    James 39
    (See also: Scarlett)
Scarlett, John 30, 42, 45
    (See also: Scarlet)
Scott, John 44
Searcy 29
    William 10(2), 19(2), 46
Seizmore, Ephriam 11
Self, Edward 20
Sellars 39
    James 39(2)
    Sampson 45
    (See also: Sellers)
Sellers, James 41, 44
    Robert 43
    Robt. 44
    Sampson 45
    (See also: Sellars)
Sergant, Stephen 27
    William 27
    (See also: Sargent, Sarjeant, Sarjent)
Shaddock 24
    Henry 24(3), 42
Sharemore, Peter 37
Sharp 52
    John Allen 33
    Joseph 7, 31
    Thomas 52
Shaw, Benj. 32
    Benjamin 28
    Ralph 54
    Timothy 34, 41
Shepherd, Andrew 41, 45, 52, 54, 55, 56
Sherrod, Thomas 26, 36
Shirret, Jas. 55
Simmons 26
    Henry 3
Simson, Richard 47
Sinat, Samuel 15
Sinklar, Charl's. 46

Sirrat, Allen 39
    Samuel 39
    (See also: Sirratt)
Sirratt 55
    (See also: Sirrat)
Skeals, William 44
Slater, John 27
Smith, Ambros 38
    Ann 1, 36
    Ed 34
    Edward 32, 34
    Edwd. 34
    George 43, 47
    John 1, 13, 32, 46, 50, 53
    Judge 7
    Luke 12, 26
    Thos. 19
    Zach 27
Sorral, Samuel 5
Southerland, Robert 5
Southwel, Edward 15
    (See also: Southwell)
Southwell, Edward 21
    (See also: Southwel)
Spencer, Jno. 55
Spinks, Enoch 36, 37, 42, 48
Standfield, John 8
    (See also: Stanfield)
Stanfield 30
    (See also: Standfield)
Starns, Ebenezer 41
    Isaac 46
Starratt, Benja 21
    (See also: Sterret, Stirret)
Sterret, James 24, 26
    (See also: Starratt, Stirret)
Steward, John 19(2)
    Samuel 9
    (See also: Stewart, Stuart)
Stewart 18
    Jas. 54
    John 24, 25(2), 29, 51, 54
    Samuel 51
    (See aalso: Steward, Stuart)
Stillwell, Daniel 11
Stimson, Enos 35
Stirret, Jas. 55
    (See also: Starrattt, Sterret)
Stokes 15(2)
Stone 55
    Edward 24(3), 30, 32, 33, 36, 41
    Edwd. 36
    Willm. 52
    (See also: Stones)

Stones, Edwd 29
    (See also: Stone)
Stout, Samuel 56
    Peter 53, 56
Strader, Conrad 53
Strahorn, Gilbert 24(2), 27
    (See also: Straughan, Strauhon)
Straughan, Bendal 29(2)
    Bendel 26, 29
    Richard 27, 29(2), 47
    (See also: Strahorn, Strauhon)
Strauhon, Gilbert 16
    (See also: Strahorn, Straughan)
Striplen, Thos. 38
    (See also: Striplin)
Striplin, Thomas 41
    Thos. 44, 56
    (See also: Striplen)
Stroad, John, Junr. 6
    Mattw. 56
    (See also: Stroud)
Stroud, John 3, 6, 17
    John, Jr. 6, 17, 25
    John, Sr. 21
    Joshua 15, 21, 24
    Peter 45
    Wm. 55
    (See also: Stroad)
Stuart, John 18, 45
    (See also: Steward, Stewart)
Stubblefield, John 50
Stubbs, Jack. 1
    John 15
    Thomas 1, 23, 31(2)
Sullivan, Owen 2
    (See also: Sullivant)
Sullivant, Owen 4
    (See also: Sullivan)
Sutherland, Mordecai 52, 55
Sutton, Joseph 36(2)
Swaim, Jno. 44
    Wm. 44
Swansey, Henry 18
Swift 31, 35
    Thomas 31, 35
Switzer, Henry 47
Synnot 30
    Capt. 11, 36, 39
    Michael 3, 36
    Michl. 40
    (See also: Synnott)
Synnott 47
    (See also: Synnot)

Taber, John 27, 28, 34
    (See also: Tabor)
Tabor, John 1, 34
    John, Sr. 1
    (See also: Taber)
Talbert 46
    James 21, 27, 40, 41, 46
    John 41, 46
    Joseph 39, 40
    (See also: Talbot)
Talbot, Joseph 39
    (See also: Talbert)
Tanner, Joseph 26
Tapley 43
    Adam 28
    Hosea 28, 33(2), 34, 411, 43, 53, 56
    Hosea, Jr. 43
Tate 48
    Robert 48
    Robt. 47, 55
Tatum, Edward 15(3), 20
Taylor 31, 50
    Arthur 41
    Edward More 33(2), 34
    Hugh 22
    James 2, 7, 9, 31
    Jas. 6(2), 20
    Wm. 15
Teague, Abraham 51, 54
    Edward 29, 30
    Edward, Junr. 50
    Edward, Senr. 50(2)
    Elijah 50
    Moses 51
    William 29, 30
Teat, Joseph 5
Temple, Samuel 16
Terrel 30
    John 24
    Robert 25
    Soloman 30(2)
    Timothy 8, 29(2), 40, 45
    (See also: Terrell, Terril)
Terrell, Obediah 22
    Robert 30
    Timothy 8
    (See also: Terrel, Terril)
Terril, Soloman 48
    Timothy 48
    (See also: Terrel, Terrell)
Terry, David 35, 40
    Stephen 49
Tharp, John 45
Thomas, James 26

Jno. 47
John 32(2), 36, 45
Owen 26
Thomason, William Turnor 42(2)
    (See also: Thompson)
Thompson, Ginnins 52
    Robert 49(3)
    Robt. 55
    (See also: Thomason)
Thonody, Vendorgrove 53
    (See also: Konody)
Thrasher, John 43
Tillet, Giles 38, 55, 56
    (See also: Fillot, Tillot)
Tillot 26
    Giles 24
    (See also: Fillot, Tillet)
Tollens, Hugh 8
Tomerlinson, John 48
    (See also: Tomlinson)
Tomlinson, William 25
    (See also: Tomerlinson)
Torintin, Alexander 29
    (See also: Torintine, Torrington)
Torintine, Alexander 16
    (See also: Torintin, Torrington)
Torrington, Alexr. 39
    Samuel 30, 39
    (See also: Torintin, Torintine)
Trice, Edward 20, 45
    James 16
Trolinger, Adam 46, 51
    (See also: Trollenger, Trollinger)
Trollenger 52
    (See also: Trolinger, Trollinger)
Trollinger, Jacob Henry 21
    (See also: Trolinger, Trollenger)
Trout, George 21
Tucker, Thomas 35
Umphries, Griffin 32
    (See also: Humphrays, Humphrey, Humphreys, Humphries, Humphys)
Usery, John 38
    (See also: Usrey, Usury)
Usrey, William 19
    (See also: Usery, Usury)
Usury, John 44
    (See also: Usery, Usrey)

Utley, John 51
    (See also: Utly)
Utly, William 42
    (See also: Utley)
Vahn, David 49
    (See also: Vaughan, Vaughn)
Vandegriff, Chris. 55
Vandegrove 55
Vanderpool, Abraham 25
Vandike, Henry 4
Vanhuck, Lawrence 27
Varnel, Wm. 30(2)
    (See also: Varnell, Vernal, Vernall)
Varnell, William 30
    (See also: Varnel, Vernal, Vernall)
Vaughan, George 15
    (See also: Vahn, Vaughn)
Vaughn, Daniel 47
    (See also: Vahn, Vaughan)
Vernal, William 32(2)
    Wm. 34, 35
    (See also: Varnel, Varnell, Vernall)
Vernall, William 8
    (See also: Varnel, Varnell, Vernal)
Vernon, Willm. 29
Vestal, David 37
    (See also: Vestall)
Vestall, William 16
    Wm. 8
    (See also: Vestal)
Wade, 1, 20
    John 6(2)
    Thos. 30
Waggoner, Henry 20
    (See also: Wagner, Wagoner)
Wagner, Henry 17
    (See also: Waggoner, Wagoner)
Wagoner, George 20
    (See also: Waggoner, Wagner)
Waldrop, Michael 36, 42(2)
    Michal 24
    (See also: Waldrope)
Waldrope 34
    (See also: Waldrop)
Walker 25, 52
    Benjamin 25
    Jno. 55(2)
    John 20, 51, 52, 55
    Moses 48
    Saml. 19, 25
    Samuel 19, 21, 43

Walker (Cont.)
    William 41
Wallace, Josiah 16
    (See also: Walliace)
Walliace, Josias 36
    (See also: Wallace)
Walter, Jacob 31
Walton, Nathaniel 25, 28, 31
    Nathl. 51, 55
Ward 52
    Benjn. 36
    Nathan 7
    William 13
Warrin, Henry 21, 34
Warson, Henry 29, 31, 39
Watkins, Jas. 46
Watson, James 2, 3, 5, 48(14),
        49(16), 52(3), 54(2), 55
    James, Jr. 52, 55
    Jas. 5, 34, 40, 48(2), 49(2),
        50(2), 51
    Moses 4
    Mr. 39
    Nathaniel 51
Watts, Wm. 20
Webb 46
    James 44, 47
    John 35
Welborn, Thos. 35, 43
    Wm. Jr. 46
Weldon 20
    Daniel 10, 32, 36
    Danl. 32
Wells, Joseph, Jr. 3
    Robt. 54(2)
West, Alexander 8
    John 8
    John, Sr. 2
    Richard 48
    Soloman 55
Wharton, William 33, 34(2)
    Wm. 41
Wheant, Joseph 55
White, Jno 41
    John 31(2), 32(2)
    Joseph 38
    William 27
    Wm. 55
    Woolrick 31, 46
    (See also: Whitte)
Whitehead 39
    Amos 39, 48
    Robert 50, 51(2)
    Thos. 29
Whitman, John 51

Whitte 47
    (See also: White)
Whitton, George 1, 36
    Robt. 46
    Thomas 49
Wierman, Nicholas 31
Wiley 34
    Hugh 17, 21
    Thomas 1, 27
    Thos. 7
    William 16, 20(2), 30, 44, 52
    Wm. 55(2)
    (See also: Willy)
Wilkins 27
Wilkinson, James 6
    Jas. 6
    Thomas 10
    William 1
Willet, Jas. 53
Williams, Arthur 50
    Benjn. 48
    Charles 45
    Daniel 18
    George 43
    Jas. 6
    Jno. 6
    Jonathon 49
    Thos. 54
    William 15, 44
Willis, Henry 36
    Prid 41
Willson, Archillus 35
    Peter 55
    (See also: Wilson)
Willy 28
    Thomas 9
    Thos 24
    (See also: Wiley)
Wilson, Archalaus 10, 20
    Archalus 28
    Archelus 20(2)
    Archillus 34(2)
    Hercules 28
    James 20
    Robert 20, 22
    Robt. 36
    William 34, 43, 54
    (See also: Willson)
Winborne, William 22, 25
Wireman, Nicholas 15
Wiris, John 16
Witty, Robert 44
Womack, Jacob 33, 35(2)
Wood 38
    Bracket 53(2)

    Hugh 24(2), 28
    Hugh, Overseer 24
    John 9, 39
Wooddy, John 19
Wooten, George 37
Wright, John 29
    Jos. 9
    Joseph 30, 54
    Michael 1
    Wm. 30
Wrightman 33
Yancey, James 43
Yarborough, Zachariah 15, 19, 25
Yarbrough, Samuel 34, 35, 45
York, Joseph 25
    Seymore 15
    Simon 15
Young 14
    Mr. 45
    Ruben 46
    Wm. 29, 56
Youngblood 53
    Jacob 8, 49
    Jno. 53
    Peter 1(2), 13, 28, 31, 51,
        53, 55
    Peter, Jr. 38, 44
Younger, James 9, 23
_____, Chas. 46
____ight, John 1
__ultman 54

www.ingramcontent.com/pod-product-compliance
Lightning Source LLC
Chambersburg PA
CBHW060517300426
44112CB00017B/2711